Too Deep for Tears

Francesca Nield

Too Deep for Tears.
Copyright © Francesca Nield 2016

All rights reserved.

ISBN: 978-1542924986

Cover photo copyright Ross Fielding
"Early Morning Dew in Tatton Park, Cheshire"

Formatting by Rebecca Emin

Cover design by Avalon Graphics

'. . . the meanest flower that blows can give
Thoughts that do often lie too deep for tears'

Wordsworth

For Alistair and Rachel

To. Alistair

love

mum

x

Acknowledgments

I would like to acknowledge Professor Carys Bannister, consultant neurosurgeon at Booth Hall Children's Hospital in Manchester, for instilling in me in those early grief-stricken days the belief that my son Gregory's short life was valuable and not in vain even if I could not at that time see it; and who initially inspired me to write this book and to seek a purpose for his life. A doctor well respected with patients; a globally acknowledged specialist neurosurgeon and researcher, she demonstrated extraordinary compassion, giving generously of her time not only to listen to our feelings, but also to patiently explain difficult medical issues in layman's terms that we could understand.

I would also like to acknowledge Mr Paul Donnai, consultant obstetrician at St Mary's Hospital for women and children in Manchester, for ensuring the highest standards in the ante natal care and the personal and safe delivery of my other children - my son, Alistair, and daughter, Rachel.

I am indebted to Leslie Keegan from AvMA for the intellect, professionalism and skill shown in assessing the legal situation. He not only helped to clarify our thoughts, but also showed immense compassion in understanding the humanity of the situation and the grief we were suffering.

Finally, last, but not least, I would like to thank my husband, Ross, for sharing difficult times, as well as good. Thank you for your enduring love and support.

Foreword

I was greatly honoured when Francesca asked me to write a foreword to *Too Deep for Tears*. Gregory and his family have lived in my memory for nearly twenty years. They, like so many other families that I have cared for as a Neurosurgeon, have had to confront the pain and sadness of conceiving and bearing a child with one of the most severe congenital abnormalities that can afflict the human body.

So many emotions are generated by the situation: great sorrow and regret for the child that never grew up to fulfil the expectations that every family has for their unborn or newborn child, and a lasting sense of loss that the person they imagined and planned for is not with them; as a baby, toddler, child, teenager and eventual adult. Alongside the hurt and pain is a great sense of injustice and anger: why did this happen to such a longed for and loved child? There is no easy answer to this question, yet over the passage of time families who have had to experience this ordeal have told me that no life of a dead baby or one who lived for only a short time has been in vain.

I so well remember one family whose extremely premature baby clung to life for a number of weeks before dying. The family learned whilst the baby was in hospital to care for him with minimal support from the nursing staff. They told me years later that their son had lived so that they could offer support to other families whose disabled children had survived but needed expert respite care – which they are now able to provide in their family home, using the skills learned during the time that they and their son spent in hospital.

And, there are so many others like them who tell similar stories.

No one can feel the pain and sorrow experienced by others but one can learn from those who have suffered. During my time as a doctor I have listened to my patients and their relatives, and I have tried to put into practise what they have taught me, what has helped them to come to terms with what has happened to them, and how they have learned to cope with the turmoil in their lives. Thus I found that very few patients come alone: most are part of a *patient* family; the parents are usually the ones most immediately involved, but other family members are also important and may have different needs and different emotions, and they too have a right to be listened to and their feelings taken into consideration.

What may not be so obvious is that the patient has an even greater 'extended family' comprised not of relatives but of those involved in their care, the medical and nursing staff and therapists, many of whom make lasting bonds with the patients. Some of my young doctor colleagues and many of the nursing staff would try to hide their emotions at the loss of a patient. I always told them that they shouldn't hide them, for if they didn't care, and care *deeply*, then they shouldn't be pursuing their chosen career. In my opinion there is no room in medicine for the 'stiff upper lip' approach of the detached unemotional doctor and nurse.

Francesca has very courageously explored the emotional rollercoaster that she has experienced since the life and death of Gregory. Others who may not be able to express their emotions in such an open fashion, and who may not have been able to analyse their feelings to the depth that Francesca has, should gain comfort from the fact that they are not alone in what they are feeling, and after reading this book they should have a greater understanding of what they are experiencing. This book would not have been written without Gregory, and if it brings comfort to only one person, then Gregory's life will not have been in vain.

Carys Bannister OBE
Consultant Neurosurgeon

From Naivety to Pain

As any new mother holding their baby for the first time, I held him gently, scared by his fragility. I cuddled him, feeling overwhelmed as I looked at his beautiful face. My fingers lightly caressed his cheek as a shimmer of sunlight from a weak November afternoon sun highlighted his perfectly formed features. Ross hovered by the side of the bed, desperate to hold his son.

I felt selfish, greedily taking in his beauty, *wanting to keep him to myself*. A nurse popped her head round the door to see if we wanted anything. *I* had everything I wanted in my arms.

'We are fine,' I told her. 'Just look at how peaceful he is.'

'He is very grey,' she replied gently.

It was then that Ross took him from me and buried his face in his tiny body, kissing him and crying at the same time. Very calmly I picked up the camera with which he had been taking photographs of us moments before and snapped father and son together.

'He is *dead* Fran,' he choked.

I already knew, but an involuntary shudder racked my body. I stared out of the window, not seeing anything. I sat impassive on the hospital bed, feeling *nothing*. No tears coursed down my cheeks as they did my husband's.

I had no tears in me. I felt nothing. I was numb with shock.

After the past few days it was a *relief* to feel this way. The rollercoaster of emotions which had seemed to be beyond human endurance, but which had become our lot, had left me bereft of emotion. I was pleased to feel *numb*. I felt that if anyone touched me at that moment I would shatter into a thousand tiny pieces; as though every living part of me had been drained from me and all that was left was an empty shell, which would shatter if touched.

Ross's father and brother popped their heads round the door, but quickly withdrew. No words were spoken.

No words would have been adequate.

There it was; the culmination of nine months of preparations, plans and excitement. It was an outcome I couldn't have imagined, not even in my wildest dreams. Even those occasional pessimistic thoughts that mothers-to-be experience about there being something wrong with the baby could not have prepared me for the nightmare of the last few days.

I took Gregory from Ross and clung to him, as a child might a favourite teddy. Although four days old I hadn't cuddled him properly, or even had him to myself; not even for a few minutes. *I was not going to give him up now.*

But I had to.

As he had died his bowels had emptied of meconium, which had escaped his nappy, and he and Ross were covered in the black sticky substance. The nurse who had looked in earlier, and had peeped through the curtain across the door throughout - on hand to help - appeared again and persuaded me to give Gregory to

Ross, to let them clean him up, promising to bring him back immediately.

I waited impatiently now, propped up on the hospital bed against pillows labelled 'North Manchester Health Authority Hospital Linen.' I felt bitterness creep into my heart then. In the urgency of the situation, they had brought Gregory in to us to die dressed in clothes donated to the hospital. Previously all he had worn on life support was an oversized nappy. I thought of all his clothes waiting for him at home, neatly organised in wardrobe and drawers, of all the love and effort that had gone into the preparation of his nursery.

An icy feeling of bitterness clutched at my heart.

As we left the hospital later that evening, leaving behind our son, another feeling descended upon me, almost forcing me to my knees. Scarcely able to walk from having had a caesarian section, I now became aware of another burden. It was as though I was carrying a heavy weight on my shoulders. I recalled my Roman Catholic upbringing, and remembered how I had felt as a child when told stories from the Bible and how I had tried to *imagine* how Jesus had felt carrying the cross, and I thought that this must be how it had felt.

It was such a physical feeling that I might have had a set of actual weights slung across my shoulders. As each pan of the scales lifted and dropped on alternative shoulders, a *myriad* of thoughts swamped me. I was leaving behind in the hospital a baby who had he lived I felt *would* have caused us a lifetime of sorrow and pain; but also one who we had expected to have brought us a lifetime of joy and happiness.

As we passed the waiting room I saw my father and one of my brother's, but couldn't acknowledge them. Ross spoke briefly to my father. He told me bitterly, which was so out of character then, that my father was waiting for a priest to arrive. Gregory had not been formally baptised. As I saw the pain and guilt of religion etched on to my father's face, it was all I could do to refrain from calling out to him to leave my baby alone: because after all, I thought wearily, what did it matter now? The nurse had told us on leaving that they might have to perform a post mortem on our son's body. The child I had loved and carried for the last nine months was no longer mine.

He was public property now.

If previously I had rejected Catholicism as a religion that controls through guilt, then at that moment I rejected *all* religions. There was *no* God, no spiritual being who I felt could have let a baby suffer the way mine had. There was no afterlife. Although I had always questioned the religion I had been taught to follow, in that moment I felt sure that I was an atheist. And, that was what I wanted to be.

I wanted *finality*, *peace* - space stretching into infinity - *nothingness*, not only for Gregory, but also for myself. Instead I seemed to be carrying a burden, a burden that I would now have to carry forever. *My guilt*. In the depths of despair over the previous days, I had planned that if I ever got my son home and *I* judged his

4

quality of life to be so poor that it wasn't worth living that I would have to put an end to his misery.

And now I would have to live with this thought forever.

Making Decisions

I was 31 years old, Ross a couple of years older. In the last year or so, I had become aware of the biological clock ticking. Although couples were now having children later in life, if at all, I felt instinctively for some reason that time was beginning to run out for us.

I was the oldest girl from a poor Catholic family, with six children. It had been a difficult childhood. Our parents were young, both from troubled backgrounds, and there was a lot of sibling rivalry. I had left home at the first opportunity to go to college. At eighteen I was sure that I was never going to have children. Growing up, I was insecure in all relationships, feeling burdened by responsibilities for siblings; and, being force fed Catholicism – at home, school and at church, I did not want to take on any other responsibilities ever ... a situation not appropriate to discuss here.

All I will say, was that I was fearful of repeating patterns seen in childhood: to the extent that - at that time, I not only didn't *want* children, but doubted that I could *properly* love a child.

Ross was also from a working class background, but as an identical twin had always had a great ally and confidant in his brother, Lee. They were very close when we met and have remained so throughout life. Their parents, grandparents and innumerable great aunts doted on them. In appearance they were indistinguishable, and as their mother chose to dress them in the same clothes, they attracted attention – invariably unwanted, wherever they went.

We met when we shared the same *digs* at college, where I was studying journalism, and Ross chemistry. Ross pursued me from the outset, but I was less keen to embark on a relationship, wanting to enjoy my new independence! Eventually, my resolve faltered and we spent many years *living in sin,* as my parents called it, before eventually getting married. The one concession to my independence was to retain my own surname, a practice more common now.

We moved frequently to study or for work, living at various times in Preston, Manchester, South Wales and London. We bought our first place in what was then a very run-down part of Fulham in London, a grotty room on the second floor of a very grim, dilapidated building in Wandsworth Bridge Rd; boastingly described by estate agents as a *pied-a-terre*! It was the smallest, grottiest 'storeroom' imaginable - over the back of a tile shop; and not even properly converted. With a sofa bed as seating and for sleeping, with the tiniest bathroom with hand basin, toilet and corner shower, a galley kitchen, where the fridge door touched the wall opposite when opened, there was no question of us starting a family there, although by now we were gradually warming to the idea.

Struggling for a miserable three years in these cramped conditions, with no money for breaks or luxuries, we sold the room for double what we had paid for it. This allowed us to take out a mortgage on a three bed semi with gardens in Knutsford, a market town in the heart of Cheshire. We threw ourselves into enjoying this home and set about getting it as we wanted it.

I now worked from home as a freelance editor, having built up contacts in London, and Ross was employed as a scientist at Ilford, a photography company in Mobberley, which specialised in black and white film.

All in all life could not have been better. We spent all our spare time travelling, walking, eating out, and exploring far-flung country pubs.

Nonetheless, it was becoming more obvious by the day that there was something missing.

There was a distinct *gap* in our lives. Eventually it dawned on us what it was. By the time we had decided that we wanted to have a family we could not imagine life without one.

As with so much in life, things did not go exactly to plan. I had expected to conceive immediately, and it was frustrating each month to find that I had not. I had spent a large part of my life trying not to get pregnant, and now that I wanted to, it came as a shock each month to find that I was not. We began to worry that one or other of us was infertile.

After six or seven months I could scarcely contain my excitement as I stood waiting to pay for a pregnancy testing kit. We were overjoyed when the urine sample revealed that I was expecting a baby.

I registered my pregnancy with a locum at

my local surgery, as my GP was herself on maternity leave. The locum told me that standard procedure was to share care for the pregnancy between the local GP and a hospital consultant. As I had no knowledge of any of the obstetricians or hospitals in the area I chose the only female obstetrician working in the specialty, feeling that she would be *empathic*, and this was the letter that was sent to Mrs A.V. Scott at Macclesfield District General Hospital:

19/4/1989

Dear Mrs.Scott,

I would be grateful if you could see and book this 31 year old primagravida for confinement. Her last menstrual period was 15th February 1989 and she currently weighs 9st. 7lbs and is otherwise healthy. Blood pressure 105/70 and urine sample negative for ketones and sugar and protein.

I would be happy to share care if you think this is appropriate.

Yours sincerely,

M. McKAVANAH
(Locum)

The letter was not signed, but someone had written beneath in biro the date *22-11-89*, the expected delivery date.

My pregnancy was registered on 17 May under the number 509975 T. A midwife did this at an ante natal clinic locally. I gave her personal health details which she recorded, before she asked for consent to allow the presence of a male student nurse during some of the procedures. I signed a form agreeing to this.

The midwife registered the pregnancy by asking for personal details and then medical details, such as illnesses, allergies, immunisations and the general state of my health. She performed a blood test. Then she took a family history, asking about any relevant medical problems. I told her that my husband was an identical twin, and that the only genetic problem that I could think of was that on Ross's side of the family there had been spina bifida.

Sister Duffield was a dark haired lady with a confident attitude and she told me that my chance of having twins was no greater than anyone else's, as the twins have to be on the *maternal* side to statistically increase the chances of this.

She confidently dismissed the idea that there could be any risk of having a baby with spina bifida as it was too far back in my husband's history to count. A great aunt, Bella, had had a daughter, who she named Jenny after her sister, who had been born with spina bifida, and who had tragically died at 15 months from meningitis.

Sister Duffield reassured me that spina bifida was easily detectable anway, with an ultrasound scan and a specific test called an AFP test, which was offered routinely at Macclesfield, being carried out to detect this if I wished to have it. She told me that these two tests together *complement* each other and that I shouldn't worry about spina bifida. If I had been older I would have been offered an amniocentesis test to look for spina bifida and Down's syndrome.

For the geographical locality where I lived I was considered too young to have this test. I told her that in view of there *being* spina bifida in Ross's history that I felt that I should have an amniocentesis test to be on the safe side. She assured me not to worry about this and spent some time reiterating her view that the AFP test and ultrasound scan, undertaken at 16 weeks, were *sufficient* to pick up any problem.

I later discovered that she hadn't even made a note about the history of spina bifida, considering it to be of no significance. She gave me a form outlining details of the AFP test. This is what I read:

MACCLESFIELD HEALTH DISTRICT

EARLY DETECTION OF OPEN SPINA BIFIDA

Every pregnant woman and her husband hopes that when their baby is born it will be healthy and completely normal. Until recently, no one could tell in early pregnancy whether the baby already had developed one of Britain's most common birth defects, called Spina Bifida. In this condition the back bone does not form completely and can result in severe crippling, mental backwardness, chronic illness or death at an early age.

If they so wish, women at 16 weeks of pregnancy have a test available to them which can help discover this problem. Usually all that is needed is a small amount of the mother's blood. This is tested for a particular protein (alpha fetoprotein or AFP) and within 10 days your Practitioner or hospital doctor will have the results.

In some cases, another specimen of blood to double check the first, is requested with an ultra sound examination and if any doubt remains a fluid test (amniocentesis) is offered. If a foetus with an open spina bifida is discovered, the parents may choose to end that pregnancy and try for an unaffected child at another time. Three out of four spina bifida babies can be discovered in this way.

If you would like to take advantage of this test ask your own doctor or at the hospital for more information.

....

7 DECEMBER, 1978
10,000 reprinted 1979

MD 259

I signed the form, requesting the test.

12

Inner Peace...

If previously I hadn't felt any great sense of self worth and worried that I might be incapable of loving a child, as soon as I became pregnant it was proved otherwise. Even before I started to look pregnant, I felt different. I felt *special*. I had a secret. It was almost as though I was the first or only person to have a baby. I felt as though I was now inhabiting the realms of the grown ups. I felt completely at ease in my skin, despite my stomach distending and the skin stretching alarmingly.

I was well, although I did suffer from morning sickness, which could strike at any time of the day or night. I had become so calm that when I did vomit I didn't find it too unpleasant. Invariably I would then crave something to eat. Often this was something completely different to my usual diet. One night I woke at midnight, threw up over the bed and while Ross changed the bedding I went downstairs and made myself a sausage buttie, which I smothered in tomato sauce. As my hormones ran amok, I craved all kinds of food, from pickled eggs or onions to more sensible meals.

I felt the baby move very early in the pregnancy for a first baby. *It was as though a butterfly flitted gently inside me.* It was such an amazing feeling that it stopped me in my tracks. I reported this to the midwife at the next ante natal clinic. She told me that it was too early to experience *quickening,* and that it must have been wind. *It was not.*

Ross and I discussed what sex we would like the baby to be. Although all we really wanted was for the baby to be healthy, he wanted a boy, who he could do things with. I wanted a girl, for the same reason, but also feeling that it would be nice to have a girl in his family.

We decided not to choose a name until the baby was born and we knew its sex, although we did throughout the pregnancy discuss various names. I felt as though I was carrying a girl, but couldn't be sure. *I was though sure that my baby was going to be perfect. Everything felt so right.*

For the first time in my life I felt that I had someone who was completely mine to love and care for. And *I* felt loved and cared for. My relationship with Ross seemed to have grown even stronger, and he nurtured and cared for me and his child I was carrying.

I felt that nothing could hurt us.

We were invincible.

I would spend afternoons resting on the bed, stroking my stomach, daydreaming about what life would be like with our family. I was already planning to have more children!

We set to work with a vengeance, preparing a nursery and buying everything that we needed for a baby. I never thought that it was bad luck to make such preparations, as some prospective parents do, I felt so confident that everything was alright. *I also had confidence that I would receive a high standard of medical care.*

I was due to have an ultrasound scan on

Friday 9th June at 11.15am. Ross planned to come with me and then we would go out for lunch. We were both very excited at the prospect of actually *seeing* our baby.

We were disappointed to see that the mother who had accompanied the lady in front of me was not allowed into the room whilst her daughter was being scanned; but felt that it might be hospital policy that only partners were allowed in.

I was consequently dismayed when a surly technician asked Ross to wait outside while she performed the scan.

She put jelly on my tummy and I left her to get on with her work, recognising that she had a job to do. She said very little, but I clearly recall her complaining that the baby did not want to be scanned '*today*'. All I could think about was when she would let me look at the screen, and whether Ross would be allowed in to see his baby.

When she had finished she did allow him in to the room, briefly turning the monitor to show us our baby on the screen. She then ushered us out, barely allowing me time to wipe the jelly from my stomach. She thrust a photograph of the baby into my hands - and the event we had looked forward to for so long was suddenly all over. I wiped my stomach with a tissue in the pub toilet where we had gone for lunch.

Although disappointed by the attitude of the technician and the atmosphere, we trusted that this was because she had to concentrate fully on her work, and we decided not to dwell on it. We trusted that she had checked the baby thoroughly. All we could do now was to keep getting out the photograph and gazing fondly at the image of our child. The technology seemed incredible to us at that time. That we could actually see an image of a baby I was carrying inside me seemed like a modern miracle.

Later, after Gregory's death, I was to look at her notes. She had noted how the baby had presented, the placental site, foetal number, the box marked F.H. was ticked, BPD was 3.5cms, the box marked T.A. had a line through it, femur length was 2.5 cms and gestation was noted as 16 weeks. The box marked F.Spine was filled in with the letters NAD. No abnormality detected? No available data? I question whether in view of her attitude and comment about the baby not wanting to be scanned *today* whether she did in fact look at his spine. At the time I took it for granted that she had looked at my baby's organs, particularly the heart and brain, and that she had looked at his spine.

All in all, although slightly disappointed with the day, I felt confident that the baby was healthy. After all I had seen him or her moving about on the monitor. Nothing and no-one could spoil my happiness.

The AFP test was performed a week after the scan on 16 June. The midwife informed me that I would not be given a result. She told me to *presume* that everything was alright unless I heard to the contrary. I felt uncomfortable with this, feeling it to be bad clinical practice. I would have felt better to be told that everything was alright.

As time progressed and I heard nothing I

breathed a sigh of relief. I was utterly confident now that the baby did not have spina bifida. The original pathology report for 'Alpha Foeto Protein' read ' = 23 ng/ml'. Across the bottom of the report in bold capitals was the statement: 'NORMAL FOR DATES PLEASE INFORM LAB OF SCAN RESULT'.

...Outward Turmoil

When I had chosen the obstetrician to oversee my pregnancy and the hospital I had done so without any knowledge of them. The obstetrician I had chosen because she was a woman. Also, she worked at Macclesfield hospital, which I felt was the easiest hospital to get to should I have to get there quickly.

She ran a clinic in Knutsford to save patients having to travel to Macclesfield, approximately 12 miles away. The clinic was rudimentary, with patients sitting in a corridor as a waiting room. There was no appointment system, the clinic operating on a first come, first seen, basis.

The procedure for transporting the blood that had been taken for the AFP test, I was to find out later; and was also, I believe, poor clinical practice. It was transported to the hospital path labs for testing in a cardboard box in the boot of the doctor's car after clinic was over. It was a red-hot day when I had my blood taken, and I was later to question whether this could have spoiled the blood sample in any way.

Having had the scan and the AFP test; being monitored at the ante natal clinic, as well as by now a permanent replacement GP, instead of the locum, I was confident that I would receive a high standard of medical care. I could feel the baby's movements much more vigorously as time progressed, and I was confident that I was carrying a very healthy baby.

I shall never forget the first time that Ross

the baby was '*growing properly.*' I was delighted by this news. We were to be given another chance to *see* our baby on an ultrasound scan. But I was irritated that she should think that I wasn't able to take care of myself or my baby properly.

Although I found her somewhat intimidating and uncommunicative, I determined that I would ask her about the adverse reports I had been hearing about the hospital. She hesitated before making any comment, and when she did reply it was with a sarcastic retort that the administrators at the hospital did not seem to understand that women do not give birth at pre-planned or regular intervals. With this she clammed up, biting her lip, almost seeming as though she had said too much. I was to find this reluctance of hers to communicate a common feature in the future. I resented the fact that she didn't seem to think that what was happening at the hospital was any of my business and that she didn't seem to be treating me as an intelligent person.

Shared Happiness

The technician who performed the scan at 30 weeks had a very different attitude to the one who had carried out the16 week scan. She had a pleasant demeanour and cheerily ushered us both into her room. The concentration on her face was clear to see as she performed the scan.

Then she turned the monitor towards us, so that we could see the baby. At the first scan the baby was so small that *all* of it was visible at the same time on the screen, whereas now the baby had grown so much that only a *part* of the baby's body could be seen on the screen at any one time. She spent some time showing us various body parts, with organs being clearly identifiable. At one point we could even see tiny fingers.

Finally, she turned the monitor away from us, declaring that if we looked any harder we would see what sex the baby was which would spoil our surprise! We were happy with this as we didn't want to know prior to birth whether we were having a daughter or a son.

She then spent some time plotting the growth of the baby on graph paper, telling us that the baby was the right size for dates. The box marked '*F.Spine*' was not filled in at all by this technician. I do not *know* whether she looked at his spine. I do not recall us looking at his brain, nor know whether the technician did.

All I recall thinking was how lucky we were to get this opportunity to once again see our baby on the screen.

I had expected that pregnancy would perhaps have been a difficult time, but I really enjoyed it. That summer, carrying my first child, was one of the happiest times of my life. In retrospect I am pleased that I had that special time, little knowing what the future held, never again being able to go through a pregnancy in such a blissful state. I also comfort myself with the thought that whilst Gregory was in my womb he was nurtured and cared for. Although only of small comfort, in view of what I was to see him go through, we did have that time together, a special time, shared by us all.

After Gregory's death the memory of my happy pregnancy was to sustain us. Neither of us shall forget that time, the expectation, the excitement of things to come, but above all else, the joy of the moment. I recall sitting in the sunshine in the garden one afternoon, and for the first time in my life I felt complete happiness and satisfaction. It was a feeling I had never known before, as though the whole of life had been suspended and frozen in that moment. The thought entered my head that if I was to die, that was the feeling I would like to experience as I did so, a complete satisfaction, an inner peace, totally in touch with my thoughts and my body. How can I explain that feeling? Words seem both inadequate and clumsy.

As summer turned to autumn more rumours began to emerge about problems at the hospital. Reports of this had even reached the press and local TV stations. *The Manchester Evening News* carried an article outlining these problems. Complaints about the hospital were diverse, ranging from the fact that the facilities were inadequate, a ward having been closed, to the fact that only women in *'established labour'* were being admitted to the hospital. It was reported that there was an acute shortage of staff, necessitating babies rooming in with their mothers. It was also reported that women were being discharged as quickly as possible after delivery.

I wasn't sure what to make of this, but a few days later had the opportunity of discussing it with my midwife. I was surprised to see Sister Duffield, the midwife who had registered the pregnancy, hurrying down our garden path.

She was on an errand from the hospital. She reassured me that although there were issues at the hospital, the situation was under control. She was visiting expectant mums though to ask them if they would be prepared to return home as soon as possible after giving birth. I didn't have any real objection to this as Ross had booked a fortnight off work to help with the baby, but was uncomfortable with the notion of being asked whether I would be prepared to leave hospital before I had even *entered* it.

When Ross returned from work that evening we discussed the situation, and the possibility of changing to another hospital. We decided that it was too late now to do this, and felt that it would be better for me to deliver the baby in the hospital where I had had all my tests performed.

Although dissatisfied with the situation, all we could do was place our faith in the hands of the hospital staff and administrators. At that time we trusted that competent and experienced health professionals would be looking after us and that all would go well.

I felt well and we enjoyed the following weeks, watching the movements of the baby, an elbow or foot surfacing beneath the skin of my now very stretched stomach. *One of the biggest thrills of all was to feel the baby turn completely over.* Although so many before me had been through the same process, a completely natural event, it seemed as though what I was experiencing was unique; miraculous almost. I could hardly believe the experience. *It was the best thing that had ever happened to me.*

'Established Labour'

The last weeks of pregnancy were very uncomfortable as I am sure they are for most expectant mums. I frequently needed to go to the toilet as the baby pressed down on my bladder. I suffered dreadful indigestion; the baby seeming to occupy every square inch of my insides now. And I felt as though I could hardly breathe.

My stomach felt as tight as a drum. I could no longer feel the shape of a baby inside me, but rather, felt as though I was carrying a solid boulder around.

The penultimate week of my pregnancy was uncomfortable and tiring, but the week leading to labour was the most difficult.

To compound my feelings of discomfort, I began to feel *uneasy*. I felt concerned that my stomach felt so tight. The baby didn't seem to be moving as much and I could hardly move myself during this last week I was so large. I began to experience balance problems. Moreover, I became unbelievably clumsy.

I spent my nights propped up on pillows, unable to manoeuvre myself into any comfortable position, let alone one where I could sleep. I couldn't get in or out of the bath without Ross's help, so wasn't even able to take a bath to relax unless he was home.

I went to bed early on the evening of Tuesday 14th November, a week before the baby was due, and dozed fitfully, suffering irregular contractions - which I experienced as a hardening of the wall of the uterus - and niggling back pains. The ante natal classes had prepared me to expect these contractions, called 'Braxton Hicks,' but in the early hours of Wednesday morning I suffered a contraction that I felt as a severe *pain*, rather than a hardening.

Consequently, that morning I was optimistic that things were happening. All morning contractions came and went, but did not settle into any regular pattern. They were painful, but not regular. I prepared to telephone the hospital as soon as they settled into a regular pattern, hoping that it wouldn't be too long now.

As the morning dragged, I became concerned that what had started as niggling back pains were becoming more severe and prolonged, although not coming at regular intervals as I had been taught at classes to expect.

Ross came home at lunchtime when I was in the throes of one of these pains and immediately telephoned Sister Duffield, the midwife. When the pain had subsided I described over the phone to her what I was experiencing. She told me that she didn't think that I was in '*proper*' labour, but was puzzled by the back pains.

She pondered aloud whether I might have a urine infection. She wasn't prepared to come and visit me and told me that I ought to see a doctor if I had an infection. I felt resentful that she had been keen to see me to carry out the hospital's errand, but would not visit me now to offer any reassurance.

I quickly pulled myself together, telling myself that what I was experiencing was all perfectly natural. *Frightening, but natural.* I telephoned for an appointment to see my GP about the back pain and was given an emergency appointment for that evening with a locum. I took the precaution of taking a urine sample with me.

The doctor told me that I had the classic symptoms of a urine infection, particularly as there appeared to be blood in my urine when he tested it. He decided that it was unfortunately impossible to actually confirm that it was an infection, as all that it might indicate was that I was pregnant, *and there was little doubt of that*!

We discussed whether I should go to hospital, and I told him about some of the issues there, and that expectant mums were not supposed to go in until they were in '*established labour.*' He prescribed an antibiotic, Amoxil, and told me to see how I got on that night. He advised me that if the pain got any worse that I *should* go to hospital, telling them that I was doing so on his advice.

As the evening wore on the pain persisted. I paced up and down, feeling tearful and tired, unable to get comfortable enough to rest. On one of my pacings the pain became so severe that I banged my head on the glass in the French windows to distract myself from it.

We decided that enough was enough and that I couldn't go through the night like that.

I was admitted to the hospital at 23.05pm and was looked after by a very pleasant midwife.

Her attitude was both kind and reassuring. She examined me and my leg trembled violently as she did so. As she examined me I had a show. My temperature was 36.7, pulse 100 and blood pressure 155/95. She tested my urine but could not detect any infection. She notified the doctor on duty of this by phone; who told her to keep me in overnight for observation of the pain and blood pressure. She assured Ross that he could go home to get some sleep and promised that she would telephone him if anything started to happen.

Throughout the night this midwife tended to me in a caring manner and monitored the baby's heartbeat on a fetal heart-monitoring machine. She told me that I was having very good and regular Braxton Hicks contractions and felt that I would deliver the baby earlier than my expected date, feeling that 'proper' labour was imminent. She was kindness itself and administered Temazepam to help me get some rest and Paracetamol for the pain.

I dozed fitfully, still feeling restless, and still in pain. The midwife looked in on me at very regular intervals. At five o'clock in the morning, on returning from the toilet, I found that she had made me a cup of tea. I had been put into a side room, in which I had been told there was a one-way window, so that I could see out, but no-one outside could see in.

As dawn broke I watched through this window as the hospital began to come to life. The hospital grounds, which had been deserted, at first light now and then revealed a figure, hurrying about their business, shoulders hunched against the chill of the dawn. Not a glance was cast in my direction. I stood for a long time watching these figures, unobserved, and feeling that it wouldn't be long now before I was holding my baby in my arms.

The midwife who had looked after me through the night looked shattered when she came in to see me at breakfast, giving me more Paracetamol and telling me that she was going to *ask* Mrs Scott to come to see me as soon as she got in. Ross telephoned to see how I was, and I told him to go into work, and that I would telephone him as soon as anything happened. The severe back pain still persisted.

Another very matronly midwife had now come on duty and she popped in to see me. She left the door ajar, so that I shouldn't feel isolated by myself in the single room.

Later, I heard this midwife discussing me with Mrs Scott. I peeped out and saw them standing at the reception desk. The room was a stone's throw from the desk and I thought that Mrs Scott might pop her head round the door to see me, as I was her patient, or even come and examine me. I was consequently disappointed to see her figure disappearing down the corridor.

The matronly midwife again appeared and took my blood pressure, which was down this morning to 130/80. She clucked like a mother hen looking after a chick, tucking my bedclothes in and squeezing my hand, telling me that she was going to keep a close eye on me.

A couple of hours passed and I assumed that I was going to be seen by Mrs Scott on a ward round. I tried to settle down to wait for this but couldn't get comfortable because of the pain in my back. I was having painful contractions, but only every now and then. I was bored and uncomfortable, moving from the bed to a chair, and pacing up and down the room.

I was surprised when my next visitor was a midwife I hadn't seen before. She told me that I should go home. *Mrs Scott had instructed this.* On my way to telephone Ross, to ask him to come to pick me up, the matronly midwife intercepted me. She was shaking her head in anger, and told me that I was in no fit state to go home.

I was astonished.

This midwife was clearly angry that I was being sent home, but my obstetrician had instructed that I should.

The midwife reiterated her view that she wasn't happy with the situation and told me not to *'disappear'* as soon as Ross arrived with my clothes, without telling me why.

The next thing that happened was the appearance in my room of a very young male doctor. His entrance was hurried and he looked very cross and tired. He asked, rather irritably, why *I* wanted to see him. *I had no idea what he was talking about.* All I could do was to explain why I was there.

He sat down wearily on the edge of the bed and said that Mrs Scott had *authorised* that I should go home. I told him that I felt unwell and that intermittently I was having contractions. He replied that I should return to the hospital when the contractions came at regular intervals or when my waters broke ...

'*when you are in established labour*', he concluded.

With this he disappeared, and I was left asking myself whether it was ethical for a patient to be admitted to hospital and then discharged without being *examined* by a doctor.

I never found out why this doctor came to visit me, but assume that the matronly midwife may have asked him to.

She certainly gave the impression that she didn't think that I should be going home. As I left later with Ross she urged me to get my blood pressure checked by my GP and to take it very easy.

The events of the morning at the hospital had left me stressed, and although uneasy with what I had experienced at the hospital I was glad to get home, to the peace and quiet there.

I telephoned the local surgery and was given an appointment to have my blood pressure checked on Friday. I spent Thursday at home quietly, unable to eat, but drinking at regular intervals, which consequently led to a lot of trips to the toilet. I found that I could not urinate properly, but assumed that this was because the baby was bearing down on my bladder, so that I was visiting the loo more frequently than I needed to.

I could not get into a comfortable position to sleep, so spent the night in an armchair trying to read. This is how I spent most of the time over the following nights leading up to labour. I would leave the curtains open so that I could look out of the window, and spent *hours* looking out at the street, lit up by a street lamp opposite;

illuminating the dark shadows of the houses across the road. Every night I watched a light go on in a house opposite where the young couple there had themselves just had a baby, and thought that this would be us soon.

I kept my appointment at the surgery on Friday, and was ushered in to the treatment room by a nurse acting as a chaperone. Again it was a locum I saw. He was on the telephone when we entered and the nurse led me into a small examination room adjacent to the main room. Before I had even spoken to her she told me that I looked unwell. I explained the events of the last few days, to which she exclaimed, '*you are in slow labour!*' She decided to weigh me whilst we waited for the doctor. She had to steady me as I stumbled trying to make the small step up on to the scales. I was surprised to see that since last week I had gained *nine pounds* in weight.

I don't remember what examinations this doctor carried out, I felt so disorientated and tired. I had never seen this man before and he had never seen me. I regretted the fact that my GP was herself on maternity leave as I felt she would have been more helpful. He told me that if the hospital considered that I was fit enough to be at home *we* would have to take their word for it. After all, they were the *experts*. I do recall him telling me that the baby's head was engaged, and offering me some, what I felt to be rather banal, advice on placing bricks under the bottom of the bed to raise it to assist with my sleeping problem.

Friday night was the worst of the pregnancy

so far. I spent the night kneeling with my face buried in the back of an armchair, with backache and the occasional, but infrequent, painful contraction. Ross helped me to get into the bath in the early hours of the morning. I felt so bad that I was sure proper labour was imminent, so Ross and I went for a walk to see if we could speed things up. I leaned heavily on his arm as my stomach felt so tight and I felt so off balance. The contractions seemed to become a little stronger and more frequent.

I was dismayed when a couple of hours later they petered out altogether. I felt dizzy, sick and confused.

The waiting seemed unbearable now.

I really don't know how I got through the next few days. In retrospect, I cannot believe how unassertive I was about the situation, but at that time I was very *naive*, not having had any previous experience of childbirth. Also, I implicitly *trusted* the medical staff.

The following days seemed to pass in a haze. I didn't feel as though my brain was working properly at all. I suffered headaches, followed by flashing lights before my eyes, even losing my vision completely for short periods of time. I had never suffered headaches before. My body, already seemingly stretched to a point where I felt as though I would burst, seemed to swell even more, to gross proportions. I had a swollen face, hands and feet. The last few days saw my legs swell to the size of tree trunks. By this time I almost felt oblivious, as though I had lost my mind. *I felt incapable of rational thinking.* I felt like a block of wood. I slowly shuffled around the house, beset by numb limbs or pins and needles, grabbing furniture to keep my balance, little discriminating between night and day.

I spent moments on the bed, and large parts of the nights in an armchair, dozing fitfully. When on the following Wednesday, just before one o'clock in the morning, I again felt a bearing down sensation on my bladder, I shuffled reluctantly to the toilet, returning to bed irritably after yet another wasted visit. I had only been there five minutes when I felt what can only be described as a *popping* sensation as the membranes around the baby ruptured.

At last, I was in *established* labour.

Not only was I in established labour, but it also looked as though my baby would be born on its *exact* due date.

I couldn't wait to meet him or her.

Our Happiness turns into a Nightmare...

The relief I had felt when my membranes finally ruptured was quickly replaced by a feeling of panic as my waters gushed. I had been told by the locum GP that the baby's head was engaged and consequently didn't expect the rupture of the membranes to result in the loss of so much liquid. It was as though the wall of a dam that had been holding water had burst as my waters gushed - and gushed ... and gushed. After fifteen minutes, when there was no sign of it subsiding, and the bed was now *awash* with water, I urged Ross to phone the hospital.

He had by this time dressed and was helping to mop up the liquid with towels. I asked him to tell the midwife over the phone that I was worried by how much water there was. All my instincts were telling me that I had too much amniotic fluid. I had read that at term the amount of amniotic fluid is usually approximately one litre.

Instinct told me that I had already lost more than that, but I had no real way of knowing.

With the loss of liquid there came a release of pressure within my uterus. Although this was a relief, this feeling was quickly overtaken by the disquiet I felt at the loss of so much water.

Although Ross conveyed my message to the hospital he did not understand just how uneasy I was feeling. I asked him what the midwife had said about the loss of so much fluid and he told me that she had responded with the retort, 'Well there will be *dear*.' I didn't feel that her attitude boded well for what I was about to experience.

Ross urged me to remain calm and told me that he had put my things in the car and covered the passenger seat with plastic, sheets and towels. About half an hour had now passed and I was still trapped on the bed with no sign of the loss of fluid subsiding. We decided that we should get to the hospital now as quickly as possible.

I felt exhilarated and frightened at the same time as we left the house.

As the door closed behind me I knew that everything would be different when I next returned home. The street was still and deserted, the shadows of parked cars illuminated by the street lamps looking eerie, and, as my eyes adjusted to this false light, I noticed how each house stood solid in the semi darkness, curtains closed against the autumnal early hours, enclosing the occupants safely within.

At once I wanted to be back in my own bed, safe, warm, and not pregnant.

As so many women before me must have thought I wondered what I was doing here in this situation.

Ross drove calmly and at speed, as there was so little traffic on the road at this time in the morning. I sat with every muscle clenched as he drove along, fearing that at any minute now I would feel the onslaught of very painful contractions. When it had actually come down to it, I had forgotten just about everything I had been taught at ante natal classes about relaxing.

Now all I wanted was to be in the hospital and everything over and done with.

I relaxed a little as hedges flitted past, and we got nearer and nearer to the hospital. We passed familiar landmarks, the lights of the village of Chelford *(there are houses here. We could stop and wake somebody to phone for an ambulance for us if I felt the urge to push. Oh no, there is an ambulance strike. Please hurry Ross. I don't want to have the baby in the car. I need to be in hospital. Dear God, what have I let myself in for getting pregnant)*. We sped around the roundabout in Chelford, through a red light at Monk's Heath traffic lights, approached Broken Cross; the hospital was only a stone's throw away now.

I just knew that I wouldn't be one of those women who welcome a contraction as a step nearer to having their baby as taught at the ante natal classes. Feeling so uncomfortable just from being so wet I decided that I was going to ask for all the pain relief that I could have. I now wanted the baby born as quickly and in such a pain free manner as possible. I had had enough pain already, and now didn't care *how* the baby was born.

I just wanted it all over and done with.

Ross parked immediately outside the doors to the maternity unit, an old two storey building, situated away from the main hospital. They were locked, and as he rang the bell to summon assistance I felt a contraction strike. The pain rose to a crescendo and slowly began to subside.

It was an African midwife who led us down the corridor. She didn't introduce herself, but we were later to find that she was called Mrs N.

Another midwife scurried past, carrying what appeared to be a placenta, only half covered in its steel basin.

After a few minutes we were led into the same room that I had been in only a week before. After showing us into the room the midwife disappeared, returning some time later to admit me. We attempted to introduce ourselves, and I tried to tell her of my concern about the amount of amniotic fluid. She totally ignored my comments, telling me to get on the bed. There she busied herself with pinching my ankles and completing the admission procedures.

I responded automatically to her questions, feeling desperately upset that there seemed to be a barrier to our communication. Ross and I exchanged looks of despair. I had never felt the need to be able to communicate with someone as much as I did that night, and I have never felt at such a loss to do so. She spoke so quietly that her comments were no more than a mutter, her face implacable to our comments.

She then examined my abdomen, and, with a sonicaid, we all listened to our baby's heartbeat. After carrying out an internal examination she muttered that I had a long way to go. At this point she strapped me to a fetal monitoring machine by a belt, which she pulled so tightly around my stomach that it was immediately uncomfortable. Asking her if it could be loosened a little she retorted, 'It's for the baby's sake, *dear*.' This last word made me think that this was the midwife that Ross had spoken to on the phone.

Throughout the night we discovered that there was an invisible barrier to our communication, but it was as tangible as any real barrier.

Once I had been strapped to the fetal monitoring machine, which was recording the baby's heartbeat, Mrs N disappeared, leaving us to get on with it. Not only was I emotionally distressed, but I was also concerned on a practical level. I was having contractions and was still losing large amounts of amniotic fluid. Because I was attached to the machine I wasn't dealing very well with the contractions, or able to get up from the bed to easily change the plastic sheet, which needed constant changing as I was still losing so much water.

Ross hunted around the room for replacement sheets and found a pile of them on top of a locker in the corner of the room. He went to the door to see what the midwife was doing and was angry to see her sitting at the reception desk, appearing to be doing nothing at all. We got on with changing the sheets ourselves at regular intervals as best we could without me being able to get out of the bed. The machine which was monitoring the baby's heartbeat was bleeping loudly throughout, which we both found distressing, and so we decided to turn the knob marked 'volume' down to a more acceptable level.

Mrs N burst into the room and marched over to the machine. Ross told her that we had turned down the volume as it was distressing us. Angrily she turned it up again, declaring that she wanted to hear it from outside. I told her of the difficulties we were having getting the sheets changed whilst I was strapped to this machine, and jerking a thumb at the pile of sheets on the locker she retorted in a very sarcastic voice, 'It *is* all quite *natural dear*,' before turning on her heel and walking out.

On the verge of tears, I had never felt as frustrated or upset as I did at that moment. My contractions were becoming more and more painful and were starting to come at more frequent intervals. Strapped to the machine I felt impotent to deal with them, knowing that they were probably going to get worse and worse. Although very upset I felt so frustrated that I was unable to cry.

Ross continued to change the sheets over the next few hours, with the midwife appearing intermittently, rarely speaking. She didn't speak to us and we now made no attempt to speak to her. She just seemed to stare at the fetal monitoring machine with a *blank* look on her face. When she did decide to examine me again I told her that I was having contractions, a comment that she dismissed with the words that I couldn't be as my cervix was not dilated very much. Without offering us any help, reassurance, or even offering us a cup of tea, or anything in the way of pain relief, she again disappeared.

I felt numb with anger and frustration and couldn't even talk to Ross now.

He was in the middle of changing the plastic sheet yet again when the midwife who had looked after me through the night last week popped her head round the door. Immediately she saw what Ross was doing she rushed in. She took over what he was doing, the whole time chatting reassuringly. By this time all either of us could do was smile feebly at her.

In what was only a relatively short time, I had lost all confidence in my instincts, and felt that there must be something inherently wrong with *my* attitude. Perhaps I was creating a fuss. I had by now completely taken on board Mrs N's assertion that what was happening to me was all quite *natural*. After all, she ought to know better than me. I fell into a kind of lassitude and decided to just let the medical staff get on with it.

My body was no longer my own.

Perhaps, like so many women before me, I had become just another statistic on the conveyor belt of delivery.

I felt totally in the hands of the medical staff, and a sense of foreboding swept over me. I was at their mercy. It was so different to what I had planned. I had hoped to be able to move about as much as possible during labour. But now I felt completely trapped, at the mercy of the medical staff. I started now to just hope for damage limitation, to come through the experience with as little emotional and physical distress for the baby and me.

I was at a loss to know why I had to be on the monitoring machine for so long and why Mrs N would make no attempt to speak to us. We had all lapsed into a strained silence now, and to make matters worse my contractions had petered out.

I lay on the bed staring at the ceiling in angry resentment at how things were going. I watched as the hands of the clock, on the wall opposite, crept insidiously around its face. Ross attempted to ask the midwife if I could come off the machine at one point, and also why a light on it was going on and off. She retorted that she didn't '*think*' that it was important, and he attempted to engage me in conversation by saying that he didn't think that she *knew* what she was doing. I didn't care by this point, although I recalled from my hospital stay the week before a doctor and a midwife joking about a new machine that no-one knew how it worked.

I prayed to get through the next few hours and hope that there would be a shift change and that I might get a more empathic midwife. We were consequently surprised when Mrs N returned to the room only ten minutes after previously visiting.

There now appeared with her, a young, dark haired man, dressed in trousers and jumper, with very dark and pronounced stubble on his face. Again we were not introduced to him, but as he said that he was going to perform an internal examination, I *presumed* he was a doctor. I was quite impassive as he examined me and told me that I was only 2cm dilated.

With this new person in the room I regained some assertiveness and told him of my anxieties. He listened carefully and decided that to ease my situation that they would fit a fetal scalp electrode so that the baby could still be monitored, but I would be able to move about more freely. He removed the belt strapped around my stomach, to reveal angry red lines where it had pinched the skin. He sent the midwife off to get the electrode.

When she reappeared she *thrust* it at him. I noted that her attitude towards him was the same as it was towards us. He returned the electrode to her and asked her to fit it, 'as I have never fitted one before.' I presumed at that point that he was a junior doctor obtaining work experience in different hospital departments.

We were shocked by what happened next.

The midwife pushed the electrode back at the doctor, whose eyes now seemed to be pleading for her help. The next few minutes were spent arguing, with them pushing the electrode back and to each other. Finally the midwife angrily thrust it at him one last time, shouting at him that it was time he *'learned'* how to fit one. The doctor by this time was visibly distressed. I was very upset.

I could hardly believe that the midwife could be so callous. It defied everything that I believed a person would enter the medical profession for.

I was not surprised that the doctor's first attempt to fit the electrode was clumsy, and for me painful.

My heart froze. My mind closed down to what was happening to me. He struggled and attempted to fit the electrode several times without success. As his dark head bent over me I coldly thought that I could punch his face. I knew that what was happening to me was not his fault, but I felt degraded and dehumanised.

He did manage to fit it, but he was pale and

had tiny beads of sweat on his face by the time he had done so. There sprang into my mind an inkling of pity for this doctor, for although he would not now look me in the eye, I felt that he felt as humiliated as I did. I believe that the midwife had brought about the situation and I found her attitude *incomprehensible*.

They then attempted to fit the electrode to the fetal monitoring machine. It didn't fit this machine. The doctor told Mrs N to go and get the machine that the electrode *would* fit. She wheeled in another, and the first machine was pushed to one side, printout, wires and belt, adding to the debris of sheets and my things cluttering the room. Neither the doctor nor Mrs N could get the electrode to fit this machine, and Ross also went to see if *he* could help. The next words I heard spoken were, '*it must be incompatible*,' followed by the doctor telling Mrs N to go and get an electrode that *did* fit the machine.

She stormed back into the room, clutching a bag, which she angrily tore open as she reached my bed.

The contents of the bag scattered all over my body. I saw Ross clench his fists very tight. I could tell that he was very *angry*. I became *numb*. I felt as though I didn't have the capacity to feel anything any more.

The bag contained what we believe were round ECG *heart* electrodes. We recognised them because Ross had had such a device attached to him when he had an operation. Throughout our son's short life he had one attached to him, so over the following days we were to see them frequently. The hospital was to later deny that this incident could have taken place, telling us that heart electrodes were not kept on the unit. I believe they were telling lies, and if not, why are heart electrodes not kept to hand?

A feeling of hysteria was now beginning to well up inside me. I wanted to scream, but was trying to rationally work out what I could do. I decided in an instant that I had to leave the hospital and go to another one. I hadn't noticed that the young doctor had disappeared.

He now returned with another man.

In a glance he took in the debris now scattered all through the room. He trod cautiously, avoiding leads and wires from the machines. As his eyes lingered on the machines I understood that the young doctor had used his commonsense and had got a technician in to sort out the machines. I became more convinced of this for although I was sure that in a glimpse he had taken in the fact that there was an electrode attached to my baby's scalp, but dangling freely, doing nothing, he did not stare at me. Instead, easing himself gently onto the edge of my bed, he took my hand and introduced himself to me by both his Christian name and surname.

I was grateful for the contact. For the first time since entering the hospital I felt as though I was being treated like a human being. He studied the printout as I asked, 'Are you a technician? Have you come to sort out the machines?' A look of surprise, then amusement crossed his face. He chortled as he responded, 'I am a *doctor*. We don't let the *porters* deliver babies in this hospital.' I thought very bitterly, *well you might as well. They might do a better job than these two so far.* I knew that what had happened wasn't his fault but I was now overwhelmed by bitterness.

He held my hand and beckoned Ross over whilst he explained that the baby's heartbeat *had been dipping all the time* and that it was *'imperative'* to speed up labour. I was immediately put on a drip to do so. I could not *believe* that the baby's heartbeat had been dipping and struggled to understand what he had just said, and why the midwife had just left us in that situation *for so many hours.*

She had disappeared completely now.

No sooner was the drip set up than the whole situation changed.

The atmosphere in the room became electric. The air seemed to buzz with tension. The doctor looked very grave as he said in the most reassuring way he was able, 'I think we will section you mum, just to be on the *safe side.*' I could not take in what he had said. I was still struggling to come to terms with the fact that the baby's heartbeat had been dipping. Ross was to later tell me that the water I had been losing was stained black with meconium, a sign that the baby is suffering fetal distress.

Suddenly, I *realised* what he had said. All that I could think was, *thank goodness. I want the baby to be born as soon as possible now.* Mrs N had completely disappeared from the scene.

The situation became frantic. The doctor rushed off to prepare himself for theatre and all kinds of medical staff started to rush in to prepare me. Ross stood by flabbergasted.

He could not comprehend how the situation could change so quickly, from the midwife seeming so lackadaisical, seemingly quite unconcerned and blasé, to it suddenly becoming an emergency situation.

I switched onto a different level of consciousness. It was almost as though I was now an observer of the scene, not a participant. I observed as a catheter was inserted into me, and as a midwife I hadn't seen before rushed in with a theatre gown. She fumbled with the gown and I noticed that she was shaking. I felt very uneasy about this. It wasn't just her hands that shook. Her whole body was shaking, even her face was quivering. I knew that the situation was serious. As she helped me into the gown her trembling body reverberated against mine.

A tiny pill cup with some pink liquid was thrust against my lips. *I* was now trembling, so much of it spilt down me. I was lifted quickly onto a trolley, as a myriad of thoughts entered my head.

Thank God, it will be over soon. I will soon have my baby in my arms. I will be spared any further humiliation. What will the baby be like? Will it be a boy or a girl? Will it be alright? Please God, let my baby be alright? Will I be properly anaesthetised. Please don't let me not be properly anaesthetised. Don't let me feel the pain, but not be able to tell anyone.

All these thoughts whizzed around in my head as I was wheeled out of the room. I saw a man, who looked as though he had just come in from outside, removing his jacket as he ran down the corridor. I knew in an instant that it was the anaesthetist. He ran ahead of the trolley, which jumped and jolted as the staff ran with it to the lift.

As new faces greeted the trolley upstairs one of them spotted that I was still wearing my rings. My fingers were so swollen that they couldn't be removed. Sticky tape was produced to cover them. I had told the midwife on admission that I was allergic to sticky tape, but already a large quantity had been bound round my arm to keep the needle for the drip in place.

I was run into the ante-room to theatre and staff awaiting me in the area, which anyone who had not scrubbed up or was wearing sterile clothing could not enter, had another trolley waiting for me.

The idea was that the two trolleys interlocked and the patient would be transferred to the theatre trolley. The staff outside the sterile area jammed the trolley I was on against the theatre trolley and I felt my baby jump with the jolt. I heard the panicky comment, 'it's been brought in the wrong way round' at the same time as I saw a man, gowned for theatre, his hair covered with a theatre cap appear. He irritably commanded, 'turn the trolley round and push it in the right way.'

At the same time someone appeared waving a consent form, screeching, 'she hasn't signed the consent form.' This was now thrust under my nose. As they tried to turn the trolley, from my prostrate position I tried to sign the form and began to feel dizzy, as lights seemed to flicker and dance, someone else screeching that it was impossible to turn the trolley around as the corridor was blocked with hospital equipment.

With a jolt I was clumsily transferred to the theatre trolley, Ross relinquishing my hand, which he had been holding, as in a small voice I tried to whisper that he wasn't to worry.

I had been delivered into the hands of the assistant anaesthetist, who leaned over me, stroking my cheek, asking me my name. He cooed and stroked my hands and face, calling my name and calling me *sweetheart*. I think that I felt a needle scratch the back of my hand, but cannot be sure. I recall a mask being placed over my mouth and beginning to feel sleepy. I think that my very last thought was that I hoped that I would be fully anaesthetised before I was cut open.

... Which goes from Bad to Worse

As I was being anaesthetised, Ross was feeling very shocked and lost. A midwife told him gently that there was nothing he could do now but wait and told him that there was a waiting area at the end of the corridor.

He reluctantly made his way there, turning back to look at the double doors to the operating theatre which were firmly closed now. The waiting area was in fact just at the end of the corridor, close to the Special Care Baby Unit, which did not arouse his curiosity as he entered the small screened-off area. It wasn't a room in any sense, but was merely part of the corridor where two chairs had been placed, with a screen for privacy. He looked at this but decided that he could not settle and he returned to the doors of the theatre. He spent some time just staring at the doors, wondering what was going on inside, knowing that to do so was fruitless, but not knowing what else to do. He looked at his watch. He had been told that the operation would probably take about 45 minutes.

Ten minutes had elapsed. He put his ear to the door and heard the clink of instruments, the sound of voices and shuffling of feet. This he found encouraging, feeling that if he could hear this then he would certainly hear the baby *cry* when it was born. With a mounting sense of excitement, but *mixed also with a sense of foreboding*, he waited and listened for the cry of his son or daughter.

The same noises persisted as more time elapsed. He still waited for the baby's cry, but it didn't come; and he took to pacing the corridor. Twenty minutes had now elapsed, and he was concerned that he still hadn't heard the baby cry. After a few more minutes he found the tension unbearable, and decided to go downstairs and outside for a smoke. He retraced his steps to the reception area, outside the room I had been in, and was asked by a nurse whether he wanted a cup of tea. He declined, telling her that he was going outside for a smoke. She asked him if he would then return to sort out my things.

He made his way to the door we had first entered; which being on a spring locked behind him. It was seven o'clock on a bright, crisp, autumnal morning as he lit up, with a feeling of satisfaction that he was at last a father, and that very soon it would all be over. As he inhaled he thought about the dawning of a new day, and with it the arrival of a new life, and decided that a baby could not hope to arrive at a better time of day. A moment of warmth and happiness surged through him, his body calmed by the nicotine, but as he exhaled a chill ran through him.

He had told himself that everything was alright, but suddenly he realised that it wasn't. He finished the cigar with feelings of mounting dread. The father of the recently delivered baby emerged to go home and exchanged a few words with Ross telling him that he had a daughter. Ross let the door spring closed behind him, and lingered awhile in the doorway, deeply breathing in the cold, fresh air.

Finally, he rang the doorbell and was let inside. He made his way to the room to tidy my things and was given a cup of tea. He began to collect everything together, which in the urgency of the situation had been scattered all around the room. The whole time he was wondering what was going on in theatre, still with the sense of foreboding. Eventually, realising that about 45 minutes had now elapsed he just stuffed everything into my bag and left it at reception.

He ran up the stairs and once more put his ear to the theatre door. He could still hear noises, but again no baby's cry. He paced up and down the corridor, feeling that it could only be a matter of minutes now before the doors opened.

As the minutes passed, five turning into 10, 10 into 15, 15 to 30, 30 into 40, feelings of anticipation, and then panic, turned into a calm numbness. He didn't know what to think anymore. He felt sick that he had not heard the baby cry. And, he wondered now whether anything dreadful had happened to me. Another half-hour passed. Ross told me that it was during this time that he began to plea bargain. He wanted us both, but as more and more time elapsed he felt sure that something was wrong. He felt mentally obliged to make a choice. He felt torn.

He wanted the baby, but he also wanted me. *Dear God*, he thought desperately. *I don't want things this way. But I* know *Fran. I don't know the baby, but I want the baby. Don't let it be her ... I know her. I don't know the baby. Dear God!*

Suddenly there were people in the corridor. One of the two doctors we had seen earlier and he could not distinguish one from the other now was walking briskly down the corridor. Ross called after him for news.

'Your baby is in the Scubu,' he informed Ross, as he hurried away.

That was all. No other information. Ross didn't know whether we had a son or a daughter, whether the baby was well or poorly, whether I had died under anaesthetic, and perhaps more importantly, in his sense of shock and tiredness, he did not know what 'Scubu' meant. Having lost a whole night's sleep, his tired mind tried to work out what this meant. He could not think rationally, and the word echoed and tumbled, over, and over, in his mind. *Scubu? Scubu?*

The doors to theatre were now open and he entered. I was in the recovery room with a tall, dark-haired nurse with a lilting Irish accent. My eyes were open when Ross first saw me again but I was out of it. The nurse vigorously rubbed the back of my hand and my cheek too, calling out my name. She asked staff emerging from theatre for my notes, but no-one seemed to know where they were. She asked Ross if *he* had them or knew where they were. He did not. She frowned, but Ross said that she seemed very efficient and kind. She did not take her eyes away from me for a second, constantly monitoring my temperature and blood pressure. A light, transparent mask covered my mouth, giving me some oxygen from a cylinder alongside the trolley, now with the sides up, so that I shouldn't fall from it.

I very gradually began to become aware of noise and light, which seemed very distant. I struggled to regain some level of consciousness. *I was frightened.* I had an awareness that I *was.* But *who* was I? *Where* was I? These were the first thoughts that began to formulate as I came around from the anaesthetic. They seemed to take a long time to form. All was confusion, light and noise, at a great distance.

Slowly, it began to come back to me, with a feeling of red-hot pain. I became aware that I was no longer *whole. They had amputated something. Terror surged through me.* What had I *lost*? What *had* I lost? I could feel where the blade of the scalpel had sliced into me, but I could not at that time *identify* the part of my body. I just felt as though some *very important part of me* had been removed. And then, *I knew. It was the baby.* The baby was *gone.* After what had seemed a lifetime of carrying the baby inside me, it was no longer there.

And I couldn't cope with the loss.

I was confused and my mind was crying out. But I was *unable* to speak. I felt as though the baby had been ripped away from me. A little voice from somewhere deep inside my consciousness began to try to form the question, *Where is my baby?* It was the hardest four words I have ever had to assemble. I was like a child trying to compose a sentence. The feeling was there, but I couldn't find the words. I rummaged around in my mind trying to pluck out the words which would make sense of it ... *baby ... my baby ... where*? And then, I had to get them into the right order. When I had composed the sentence in my mind, I tried to *whisper* it, but the words wouldn't come out. They had clarified in my mind, all lined up in the correct order, and the thought ran over, and over, in my mind, *Where is my baby? Where is my baby?* But I couldn't get the thought to connect with my mouth.

The nurse soothingly tried to bring me round. Ross said that her eyes never left my face, her gentle voice calling out to me, over and over again. Ross also called out to me. I became aware of being in the presence of someone I knew but I could not get to grips with the situation. All that I could now think of was those four words, *Where is my baby?* But it was as though I was dreaming, or in a nightmare. I couldn't vocalise them. The words were there but I was paralysed from speaking them. My thoughts were small, delimited, and my words seemed non-existent. I don't *know* whether I did eventually manage to whisper them aloud. Certainly they seemed to be coming from somewhere very deep in my mind, but I feel that I must finally have managed to whisper them because I now heard the nurse say, 'You have a baby boy.'

For Ross, other than the doctor's retort, this was the first news that he had had of the baby and his heart leapt. He joined the nurse now in trying to get the news through to me, 'We have a little boy, Fran, a little boy.' Boy ... boy ... little boy ... BOY ... a boy ... of course, a boy. Finally, the thought pierced my consciousness. *A boy.* But I was still frightened. *He had been severed from me, and I didn't know where he was.* The feeling was strange. I felt so *empty*, so *bereft*. And the words still somersaulted over and over in my mind. *Where is my baby?* I wanted to scream them out loud, but I just couldn't seem to get them out. Ross and the nurse continued to try to reassure me.

Ross felt torn. He felt that he *ought* to be with me, but he wanted to know where the baby was, wanted to *see* him, and he still hadn't worked out what Scubu meant. He asked the nurse now where the baby was, and without taking her eyes from me, she pointed and replied, 'He is over there.' She pointed in the direction of the corridor where the screened-off area was. Ross asked her whether he could go and see the baby. She replied, 'You had better not, not just yet.' He was torn. Now he regrets that he didn't just walk down the corridor and find his son. At the time he respected decisions made by the medical staff. Added to which, he said that I looked so distressed that he felt that I needed him there.

In the background now, inside the theatre, there could be heard the clang of metal buckets and the hiss of water, as though the place was being sluiced down.

It was now decided to take me to a ward. I was still not completely aware of what was going on, though I had a feeling that I was moving as the trolley was pushed down the corridor. Ross was told where I was being taken, and asked to go down the stairs to collect my things and meet me on the ward. I was taken down to the ground floor in a lift. The whole time the same sentence echoed around my mind.

By the time I reached the ward, to find Ross waiting to meet me there, I had regained consciousness a little more and recognised his rather blurred and concerned face. Two of the staff began to lift me onto the bed, and as they did so the most incredible pain seared across where I had been cut. I screamed the most horrific and loud yell of my life, which I believed would have been heard by the whole town. Ross told me later that it was only just audible and came out as a low moan. My body sagged onto the edge of the bed, so I had to be lifted again into the middle of the bed. Although I felt the same pain I had already become used to it and I don't believe I made any noise this time.

I was in the top bed on a ward that contained about 12 beds, although at this time I was oblivious to my surroundings. All that I could think about was where my baby was and I struggled again to ask in a small voice. Ross sat down at the side of the bed and took my hand, trying to calm me.

'We have a little boy,' he told me. 'I am *sure* that we will be able to see him soon.'

He told me later that he didn't know what to make of the situation, though he felt a sense of foreboding, but his principal concern at that time was to calm me. He said that I looked very pale and distressed, and that I looked all the worse because of the drip and catheter.

And so we sat waiting, trying to remain calm. An hour must have passed in this way, during which time we tried to quell our concerns. And, in a sense, we were calm. The whole situation had become totally beyond our control, and we had become almost paralysed with shock at the uncertainty of it. It was almost as though there was an electric fence around the bed. We were left completely alone, just waiting for news, not seeking any further information, and none was offered.

Ross told me that the doctor had told him that our baby was in the *Scubu* and I was able to explain that this must mean the Special Care Baby Unit. I recalled reading somewhere that all babies born by caesarean section are taken there as a matter of course, and I latched onto this explanation now, and told Ross of it. In this way we were able to reassure ourselves that everything was quite normal, that what was happening was just part of hospital procedure.

However, as more time passed we became more and more anxious. Trying to stay outwardly calm for each other, inwardly we were each wondering what was wrong. For me the whole situation was wrong. I should have been with my baby. Ross chatted reassuringly: 'They are probably just waiting for a doctor to *examine* him before they bring him to us ... it will be *something like that,*' he told me.

And the whole time that we were waiting we did expect that our son would be brought to us at any minute, or that we would be taken to see him. And so we were prepared to wait, not realising just how much time had elapsed.

Suddenly, there was a white-coated figure at the bottom of the bed, a woman. *Her appearance was fleeting, her news stunning.*

She informed us abruptly from the foot of the bed that, 'Your baby is very poorly and in the Special Care Baby Unit. Do you want him *baptised*?' I responded loudly, and in shock to this news, '*No!*' and she literally *ran* away. I think that she took my comment to be the answer to her question, but I was crying out in shock and disbelief at the news. I could not believe what she had just told us. If she was asking us whether we wanted the baby baptised, to my mind that meant that he was dying. I just couldn't cope with the idea.

And then I became angry. Where was the doctor who should have informed us of what was going on? What was wrong with our baby? Why weren't we involved? Why wasn't I with him?

This devastating news spurred Ross into action and he ran upstairs to see our son. He found him lying on some sort of table, with large plastic tubes over his body, leading to his mouth, with other tubes and wires over and around him. There was a plump lady sat at his head, on a high stool, monitoring him. Her name was Dr Shackleton, a consultant paediatrician.

She spoke to Ross but didn't look at him as she did so, keeping her eyes on the baby. She asked whether we had decided on a name and Ross replied that we had decided on Gregory, using our first choice name, there being no opportunity now to match the name to the baby.

He asked what was wrong with him and Dr Shackleton told him that she didn't *know*, that he just seemed a '*lazy*' baby. She said that he wasn't attempting to breathe. She told Ross that it looked as though he would have to be ventilated for some time, and that as Macclesfield were not geared up for this that she had decided to transfer him to another hospital to look after him, Leighton Hospital, near Crewe. A photograph was taken of Gregory and Ross returned with it to my bedside.

He was in tears as he handed me the photograph and told me that he had called the baby Gregory and that he was really beautiful. In a bid to hide his tears and to ease the tension a little he joked, 'I almost called him Geoffrey. I don't know what you would have said if I had!'

I looked at the photograph, but I could not see it through a haze of tears and anaesthesia. The photograph was blurred anyway, and as I tried to blink away my tears and clear my head all I could see was a baby's head. The features of the face were indistinguishable.

We told each other not to lose hope. At this point I thought that if all that was wrong with him was that he was a lazy baby, then perhaps this was because he had been born by caesarean section, rather than naturally, and that it would only be a short time before he began to breathe by himself. *But I was desperate to see him.* I knew where he was now, and that Ross had seen him, but nonetheless I felt that *I* ought to be with him or just *near* him.

The Special Care Baby Unit seemed such a long way away. And so we sat gripping each other's hands, feeling anxious. Suddenly another thought occurred to me. If he was going to be transferred to another hospital what was to happen to me? Would I be going with him? Would I even *see* him before he went? I felt trapped, staring in desperation at the drip and catheter.

All these thoughts were racing through my mind when a plump lady appeared at the foot of the bed. For me she was a new face, but Ross recognised her as the paediatrician, Dr Shackleton. Her face was grave as her eyes scanned my face. She asked Ross if he would come to one side so that she could have a word with him. The two disappeared completely from the ward. They were gone some minutes and I would have thought that many thoughts would have raced through my mind during this time, but none came now.

I lay in the bed frozen with terror, fearful of the news that the doctor was conveying to Ross, but unable, or nor daring, to think of what it might be.

I was to find out what it was when Ross returned a minute or two later. His face spoke volumes and I knew from his look that there was going to be no easy way to break the news. With a look of incredulity and despair he blurted out just five words, the hardest five words he has ever had to utter.

'The baby has spina bifida.'

As he said the words 'spina bifida' a terror that I felt in my stomach surged up and clutched at my throat, as real as fingers tightening around it, constricting my breathing and choking me with anguish. It was terrible but also surprising news. I had been sure that he was going to tell me that the baby had died.

'Spina bifida?' I replied. 'He *can't* have spina bifida. *I was tested for that.*'

Ross told me that Dr Shackleton had taken him into an office and had made him sit down. She had put her hand on his knee, looking visibly shaken herself, and told him that there was no easy way that she could tell him what she had to. Therefore, all she could do was to break the news to him bluntly. She told him that as they were moving Gregory to transfer him to Leighton Hospital, she *noticed* that he had spina bifida. She had then told him that in consequence of this she had had to revise her plans and that he would now have to be transferred to Booth Hall Children's Hospital in Manchester.

Ross disappeared then. He went back upstairs to the Special Care Baby Unit to have another look at Gregory. He reappeared fleetingly at the side of the bed and said,'Oh Fran, you *must* see him,' before disappearing again. He told me later that he had gone to speak to the medical staff to request that I be taken to see my son, but the staff were unwilling to move me.

I hardly noticed that Ross had disappeared I was so preoccupied with the devastating news which had just been imparted. My baby had spina bifida. And he couldn't breathe. In that instant I felt that if he wasn't breathing by now and he had such a terrible congenital defect that he would probably never breathe unaided. *All my instincts told me this*. But I could not cope with the thought. My baby should have been healthy. All my rational thoughts now fought against my instincts.

This could not be true. I tried to push my instincts away. There was nothing *wrong* with my baby. There couldn't be, *not spina bifida anyway*. It was the one thing that I had been thoroughly *tested* for. But from the back of my mind there surfaced the knowledge that Ross's great-aunt, Bella, had had a baby with spina bifida, who had suffered and died. But this knowledge conflicted with the fact that I had been tested for it; indeed, thoroughly tested in view of having informed the midwife at the booking clinic of this.

I told myself then that perhaps they had mixed up *my* baby with someone else's. After all, I had seen how inept the staff had been since I arrived at the hospital. I didn't trust them with anything now. I simply didn't believe them. This was just another in a long line of blunders. I felt frustrated, helpless from anaesthesia, exhausted by emotion, and trapped on the bed by the drip and catheter.

I pleaded with Ross now to go and find our baby. Find him and bring him to me, if indeed it was a boy. Take things out of the hands of the medical staff, I urged him. Enough is enough. We had to take control of the situation now. Our baby had to be properly looked after by those who loved him. Nothing else seemed right.

In the time that he was gone I thought about what I had asked him to do. I even thought that if it was *our* baby, a boy, who had spina bifida and he couldn't breathe, then it was imperative that he was with us, his parents. *I wanted him so much, but instinct was telling me that if he was so poorly, that if nature had engineered things this way, that if he wasn't breathing, then he was probably stillborn, and that he should have immediately been brought to us to cradle. I hated the thought of him being treated the way I had in labour. If it was our baby and he was so poorly then perhaps we would have to let him go.* I didn't *reason* why I felt like this, but just felt in that instant that perhaps that was the way it should *be. My mind and body were crying out for my baby, but instinct told me that I had to let go if that was nature's way. If it was our baby and he couldn't even breathe he should be allowed to die in peace.*

I didn't reason it all out. I only know that in that instant it felt like the right thing to do. The only thing to do. *I felt that the thought was motivated by love.* I had not as yet had time to think of the real consequences of what having a son with spina bifida might be, *for him, or for us.* It was later that I would begin to think in any depth about how spina bifida might affect his life and ours.

I loved my baby, but all my instincts were telling me that you couldn't fight nature.

My instincts were interpreted as being selfish.

I feel that they were motivated by love.

My instincts may have been *wrong.* All I know is that that is how I *felt. I was a mother trying to protect her baby.*

Ross had returned to the Special Care Baby Unit and attempted to speak to Dr Shackleton about the situation. He tried to ask her to involve us and she responded angrily, asking him if he couldn't see that she was busy, telling him to go away, and that she would come and see us when it was convenient. She appeared a short while later at the foot of the bed, and very angrily asserted 'The *baby* has rights too.'

I stared at this doctor, who had taken over all care and responsibility for *my* baby, and thought to myself: *What does she know? I was the mother of a baby, who I had carried and been so emotionally involved with for the last nine months and she was making comments that seemed to imply that I was an antagonist.*

The thought hurt me to the core.

I did not understand how she could think such a thing. Later I was to reason that her whole medical career had imbued in her that at all costs she should prolong or save life. My instincts were telling me otherwise, and it was not because I didn't love my baby.

I know that the debate about the right to life or the choice to die with dignity, and who should be able to make such decisions, is an ongoing medical issue and that there are many difficult problems to debate concerning this, both ethical and legal - but all that I can really say about this after being put into the situation we were is that the opinions of loved ones should be listened to and, at the very least, respected, even if not acted upon. After all, they are so much more *closely* involved than anyone else. Perhaps some would argue *too* closely involved to make rational decisions, but I believe that emotions should at the very least be respected.

She now told us that Gregory was being prepared for transfer to Booth Hall Children's Hospital before disappearing. I was devastated. He was being transferred to another hospital and I hadn't even *seen* him. Furthermore, I felt as though I was being treated as an antagonist.

The situation was unbearable.

All Ross could now say over and over was that I had to *see* our son.

Suddenly, I snapped. I went berserk, screaming and snatching at the drip, starting to tear off the tape that was securing the needle. I wasn't going to be prevented from seeing my baby by *anyone*. And then, suddenly, there were staff all around me, trying to calm me, searching aloud for ideas as to how I might see my baby. The difficulty was in the geographical location of the Special Care Baby Unit. I had been taken to the ground floor of the hospital, whereas the Special Care Baby Unit was on the first floor.

Previously a woman having a caesarean section would have been on the upstairs ward, whose closure was reported earlier in the autumn in *The Manchester Evening News*, close to theatre and the Special Care Baby Unit.

So many reasons were put forward for me not being moved, the principal one being that I had just had a major operation and that I ought not to be moved. Finally, with both me and Ross telling them that I *was* going to see the baby, the staff relented, and it was decided that I would be taken up in the lift in the bed to see Gregory.

The bed was pushed to the lift, with a nurse

attending to the drip and Ross carrying the bag of urine. The lift was hardly big enough to take the bed. Somehow it was got in, with those in attendance sitting on the edge of the bed, as there was so little space, though I think someone also ran up the stairs to meet us.

The bed was pushed down the corridor on the first floor until it came head on with an X-ray machine, the same equipment that had been blocking the corridor when I was taken to theatre. Someone then produced a wheelchair and I was dragged from the bed, still only wearing the operating gown, into the wheelchair. A blanket was now wrapped around me, as the gown was open at the back.

I was wheeled into the Special Care Baby Unit. *I noticed no-one other than Gregory, although there were lots of people in the room.* I didn't notice whether there were any other babies in the room. *My eyes saw only my baby, and he was unmistakably mine. I recognised him. I hadn't seen him before, hadn't been able to clearly make out his face from the photograph, and yet here I was, still only in the doorway to the room, and I already recognised him.*

I was pushed towards him, sobbing, feelings of love mixed with sorrow for this beautiful baby. *My son.* I looked at his face and he was indeed beautiful. A bonnet covered his head, wisps of downy hair escaping it. His eyes were closed but his features were perfect. He was lying on his side and I noticed he had shoulders the same shape as my husband's. One tiny hand lay outstretched on the table, closed in a small fist, the other tucked somewhere beneath him. There were tubes and wires everywhere.

I asked to be shown his spina bifida and his back was shown to me. There was a sac-like, bloody swelling there, with what looked like exposed bone. It looked large on his tiny frame - and messy; like oxtail, cut by a butcher, as yet uprepared for sale in a supermarket.

Every pain I could imagine shot through me at the sight.The pain I had experienced from my operation was *nothing* to what I now *felt* as I saw his back.

I wanted to reach out, to touch his back and soothe away the spina bifida from this innocent baby. I felt enormous bitterness and anger well up inside me at the thought of a newborn baby born with such a terrible affliction. It looked so bloody, sore and strange: like something which should have been inside his body.

All I could do was sob chokingly. Hands reached out to comfort me, and I heard someone say, 'Would you like a photograph of the two of you together?' I managed to convey that I did want a photograph, before burying my face in my hands and breaking down completely. Ross cried too.

We were introduced to staff standing by Gregory who were introduced as a flying squad from Leighton Hospital, who had come from there to escort Gregory on his transfer there. They seemed redundant now, just looking on helplessly as we were asked to leave so that Gregory could be prepared for transfer to the hospital in Manchester.

As I was pushed out and down the corridor I

felt as though I was still attached to Gregory by some *invisible* umbilical cord. As I was pushed further away I felt a physical pain at the separation. One of the nurses assisting asked me whether I wanted to go down to the foyer to watch Gregory go. I told her that I did and we went there now to await his departure. I sat in the wheelchair in the foyer feeling quite numb now, Ross still holding the bag of urine and the nurse busying herself with the drip.

A policeman entered in uniform. He looked shocked when he saw us in the foyer. Then a look of realisation came into his face, followed by a look of pity as he passed us without speaking. He raced up the stairs two at a time. I knew then that there was going to be a police escort for the ambulance carrying Gregory to Booth Hall Hospital.

It was then that I seemed to become totally detached from the situation.

I told myself that this was all just a nightmare. *It wasn't really happening.* It couldn't be. It was like watching a scene from a film or something on TV. It couldn't be real.

But sadly it was.

After 20 minutes Gregory was wheeled past us in an incubator, still connected to various tubes and wires, into a waiting ambulance. I didn't even see his face. *All* that I could see was a small bundle wrapped in what appeared to be foil in the middle of the incubator.

Our baby.

I was frozen, mentally and physically. The nurse rubbed my hands, telling me that she had to get me back to bed now. I stared vacantly into space, seeing nothing.

The whole situation seemed so bizarre that I couldn't comprehend it.

I cannot recall my journey back to the ward. But soon I became preoccupied with thoughts of Gregory's journey. I wondered which route would be taken. Would the ambulance go on the ordinary roads or take the motorway? I had no idea where the hospital was other than that it was somewhere in Manchester. I prayed that the journey would be smooth, that the roads wouldn't be *too* bumpy. The thought came into my head that Gregory might die en route and would be *alone* and I vowed that if he did I would never *forgive* myself for just letting him go. I started to think that I wouldn't forgive the hospital either. I hadn't even broached the subject, but I felt that I ought to have gone with my baby, but all my strength, mental and physical seemed to have deserted me.

As soon as I had been settled on the ward Dr Shackleton again came to see us. She told Ross that he now had to get to Booth Hall Children's Hospital himself *'as soon as possible'* because the baby would have to be operated upon and there would be consent forms to sign.

I couldn't understand why it hadn't been suggested that he go in the ambulance with Gregory, but it hadn't, and we had been too shocked to think of this. She proceeded to explain where the hospital was and told him that he had to go to Ward 14 and ask for Miss Bannister, a neurosurgeon there. She disappeared to get her copy of an *A-Z of Manchester* to help him find the hospital. On her return she suggested a route, urging him to get into our car and drive straight there.

At this urging I became angry. I had given birth to Gregory just after 7.00am and it was now 11.00am. All those hours had elapsed before Gregory had been transferred and she was urging Ross to now hurry to the hospital as though any delay by him would be damaging in some way to Gregory. I begged him not to listen to this doctor, who seemed to be putting him under such pressure, but instead to phone his parents, whom I knew would be at home as they were retired, to collect him and drive him there.

I now felt torn. I was desperately worried about Gregory, but I was also concerned that Ross did not have an accident in his urgency to get to the hospital. He was in no fit state to drive. I was surprised that the doctor could not *see* this. She didn't seem to see *anything* from our point of view.

But she must now have seen how angry I was because she went off to phone his parents for him. She spoke to his mum, informing her that I had had a little boy and was 'comfortable,' but that the baby had spina bifida and was '*poorly*' and had had to be transferred to Booth Hall Children's Hospital in Manchester.

This was how they found out that they were grandparents for the first time. They arranged that they would meet Ross at our house and that they would drive him to the hospital.

I shall never forget his face as he came to say goodbye to me.

The Longest Day of my Life ...

Before Ross left he was asked for his permission to have me sedated. He thought this over. Previously he would never have made such a decision without first discussing it with me, but knew that he couldn't possibly leave me in the distressed state that I was now in. He felt torn. He knew that he had to get to Manchester to be with Gregory, but didn't feel that he could leave me alone given what he had seen me go through.

He knew that I wouldn't be able to rest whilst I didn't know what was happening to Gregory, but another thought now sprang into his mind. He was later to tell me that he could never have imagined so much going wrong since we had entered Macclesfield hospital and he felt very bitter about this, feeling that if the staff had set out to torture us that they could not have done so as horrifically and effectively as they had. He couldn't bear the thought of me suffering any more and decided that it probably would be best if I was sedated.

I pleaded with him to be careful driving as he too was in a state and had lost a whole night's sleep.

Once sedated, I drifted heavily in a state somewhere between sleep and reality, where I neither felt properly asleep or awake. I had thoughts heavy as lead, but *vague* as I couldn't now really grasp what had happened.

It was almost as though I was drifting on

the edge of a nightmare from which I struggled to wake.

I felt at once desperate and numb.

I didn't know whether I had simply dreamed that I had had my baby, or whether I had in fact delivered him, but the blurred, hazy face of a baby hovered on the edge of my consciousness. My heart and mind seemed to cry out a name – *Gregory*.

The day passed in a blur. At times, I recall feeling lucid, at others adrift from reality. I have no recollections of the sequence of events of the day, but have memories of the events.

However, I was unaware of how much time had elapsed, or what time it was at any particular stage. When lucid, my thoughts were of Gregory and Ross. *Where were they? What was happening?* I felt desperate, then numb, then felt as though I was somewhere far away from where all this was happening, as though it was my imagination playing tricks on me. It seemed so horrific that I didn't *believe* that it could be true.

I had a couple of visitors during the day, Mrs Scott and Dr Shackleton, but have no recollection of the times or the sequence of the visits.

Mrs Scott, the obstetrician, pulled up a chair and took my hand. Her visit seemed brief, and I stared into steely blue eyes, which seemed as dispassionate as the voice which told me that my scans and the AFP test had been looked at, and that there had been no evidence from these tests to indicate that the baby had spina bifida. She did not elucidate on this and I didn't respond to her, now staring beyond her shoulder, her face becoming blank as I didn't respond. I wanted her gone from my bedside, her news and manner of imparting it of no comfort whatsoever to me.

Dr Shackleton, the paediatrician, also took my hand when she visited, now telling me that Gregory had been diagnosed at the hospital in Manchester as suffering from something else as well as spina bifida. She mentioned the name of this, a word I had never heard. She repeated the word. I *heard* it, but could not digest it, or interpret what it meant. What she in fact told me was that Gregory had hydrocephalus. I heard the word, but my brain now seemed to shut down, as though in a desperate effort to protect itself.

I heard the word, but didn't know what it meant; and furthermore now, I did not want to know what it meant. I could take no more.

I recall that she became exasperated then, shaking her head, telling me that I wasn't listening, that I was 'doolally.' This word I understood, but I was impassive to her comment. The thought even entered my consciousness that I probably did appear this way, but I knew that within the deep recess of my brain there was an intelligent, rational person. I was simply too exhausted by emotion and numb with shock to be able to vocally articulate my thoughts or want to talk to anyone other than Ross, who wasn't here.

The nursing staff didn't attempt to engage me in conversation, but performed their nursing duties quietly. They adjusted my drip, administered pain killers and emptied the bag for my catheter which seemed to fill quickly. I observed as though I was a bystander, as though none of this was happening to me.

As the effects of the sedative must have worn off, I began to feel more and more uneasy. Not only was I in pain from where I had been operated upon, but I felt a dull, heavy emotional pain also *tearing* at my insides. I became sure then that I wasn't dreaming and that what had happened was *real*, but I couldn't get to grips with my thoughts.

I noticed other women on the ward, and saw a baby in a crib alongside the bed of the woman in the bed directly opposite me. I stared at the two of them, but as though with blank eyes. No eye contact passed between us.

Unease began to well up stronger inside me. *Where was Ross? Where was Gregory? What was happening? What were the consequences of Gregory having spina bifida? How could he have spina bifida?* That was the last thing I had expected as it was the *one* thing I was sure he had been tested for.

Suddenly, the most terrible feelings overcame me. Not only did I feel bereft of my baby, I became immensely angry and bitter too. I cried out then, and a member of the nursing staff hurried over to the bed.

'How can my baby have spina bifida?' I asked her. 'I was tested for that.'

She tried to placate me by explaining that spina bifida is a common birth defect and quoting statistics to back this up, faltering when she told me that not many babies are born with this nowadays because of the testing procedures in place.

I stared at her, feeling hostile. Her face grew red at these last words and she quickly hurried away.

I couldn't believe what had happened to us. I had always, naively, thought that such things happen to other people. And I tried to understand why so many mothers had healthy babies and that I had not. I felt it as the most bitter of blows. And, I questioned why when disaster had come our way, that it had involved our baby, our newborn baby, our *first* child. I was unable to cope with any of it.

I felt then that the staff began to give my bed a wide berth and who could blame them. Perhaps they saw the wild look in my eyes, a look of disbelief, incomprehension and anger. For my part, I didn't want any of them to come near me.

With a pounding heart, more thoughts now began to seep into my consciousness, each more horrific than the last. The thoughts swamped me. I was unable to rationalise one, before another, more horrific, replaced it. The most awful one at that time was the thought that Gregory might even by now be dead.

In an effort to distract myself from these horrors I focused on the lady in the bed opposite. It was time for her to feed her baby. As she was breast feeding one of the staff pulled the curtains around her bed for privacy. I did not avert my eyes, but instead continued staring, my eyes boring holes through her tented sanctuary. After a while, I averted my eyes and looked down the ward. Numerous pairs of eyes returned my gaze, but no-one spoke. Most quickly looked away, but not before I had registered both looks of fear and pity.

There were no other babies on the ward.

In an attempt to ease the tension, one of the women, who was sitting up in bed with a scruffy jumper over her dishevelled nightdress clumsily got out of bed, impeded by her bump, telling the other women in the ward that she was gasping for a fag and was going to sneak into the toilets for one.

Hot tears coursed down my cheeks now. They dripped from my chin, joining rivulets of liquid running from my nose. I pulled the sheet up and buried my face in it.

I was trapped in my own private nightmare.

Booth Hall Children's Hospital, Manchester

On leaving me, Ross had driven home on automatic pilot. He had no better an understanding of events than I had. He knew that what had happened was reality, but felt so numb from the shock of it all that he simply couldn't comprehend it.

His parents had not arrived by the time he reached home, so he fell back on routine, performing trivial domestic duties until they arrived, even putting the rubbish out for the dustmen who were due that day.

When they arrived, his mum gave him a hug and asked,

'*Oh God!*, Ross. Whatever has happened?'

She wanted to make him a cup of tea to ease his distress a little, but he told them that there was no time to be wasted, and that they had to get to Booth Hall Children's Hospital as quickly as possible. However, their presence eased the weight he felt that he was carrying alone on his shoulders.

In the car he concentrated on studying the *A-Z* and giving his dad instructions on the best way to get to the hospital which was in Blakeley. As well as concentrating on this task, he recounted some of the events of the last few hours to his parents.

The M6 was choked with traffic and progress seemed to be painfully slow. Anxiety welled up from the pit of his stomach. This was made worse by the fact that no-one knew where the hospital was, and his dad's car was very low on petrol.

On leaving the motorway, his dad started to search for a petrol station and Ross became very upset then, urging his father to try to get to the hospital as quickly as he could, hoping that they had enough fuel to get them to the hospital, whilst at the same time trying to work out the best route to get there from the *A-Z*. They were eventually forced to stop for petrol and this simple act caused feelings of despair to rise up inside Ross.

The hospital turned out to be just around the corner from the petrol station.

He observed that it was situated opposite parkland or a common of some type, but that the landscape was bleak – as city parks often are – the bleakness accentuated by the season, trees denuded of foliage, their stark outlines silhouetted against a grey autumnal sky.

They took what appeared to be the main entrance into the hospital grounds and were faced with a central building, an old red-brick ramshackle building, probably Victorian in origin. At one time it had been an old workhouse infirmary and its structure and fabric appeared old and shabby to Ross, who decribed it later as looking as though it was crumbling before his very eyes.

This did nothing to alleviate the *terrible* anxiety he now felt.

As he got out of the car a cold chill enveloped him. It wasn't just the chill of a November afternoon which seeped into his bones. He described it as a cold dreadful feeling which seemed not only to encircle him, but to penetrate his insides. It was as though the ghosts of dead children were tugging at his heartstrings, whipping up a draught of air as they encircled him, tugging at his jacket as though teasing him, encircling him in their foreshortened play, as though they were forever trapped, haunting the place of their last repose.

The icy finger of death touched his heart.

They entered the hospital through a revolving door and made their way down a long, cold corridor, lined with murals, posters and childish paintings and drawings. Ross felt as though the very walls of the corridors were screaming at him; as though echoes of the childrens' pain and anguish were trapped there.

He shuddered, the shudder starting in his mind, then travelling through his whole body. His mum placed her arm through his as they made their way as instructed at Macclesfield to ward 14. They passed several patients on the way, but averted their eyes from them. It is difficult to confront an adult's illness; scarcely possible to face a suffering child.

Ward 14 was a neurological ward, and upon entering they were shown to a waiting room at the top of the ward. This room was to become a common feature for us all over the following days as we were to spend so much time there. They were settled by a nurse with a tray of tea and a dose of kindness to await the arrival of the neurosurgeon.

The room was shabby but warm, and in one corner was a tank containing dry twigs and leaves, camouflaging stick insects, and Ross focused his attention on this.

They didn't have to wait long before the door opened and the neurosurgeon entered and introduced herself.

Her name was Miss Bannister and Ross's mum told me that she was shocked at the first sight of this consultant. She had expected her to be an intimidating presence, possibly wearing a white coat. Instead a middle-aged, very ordinary looking lady entered. She was wearing an anorak, had snagged tights and muddy shoes. To Ross's mum she looked like a retired housewife who had come in from working in her garden.

This first impression was to quickly change once the introductions were over. She wasted no time in getting straight to the point in discussing Gregory's condition. She was calm, direct, but compassionate. Although she explained Gregory's medical problems she pitched her conversation to the level of her listeners.

She explained that Gregory needed an operation on his back to cover the open spina bifida as whilst the wound was open there was a high risk of infection. She then went on to explain that on arrival at hospital they had scanned Gregory's brain to try to determine why he couldn't breathe. She now produced images to assist her in explaining that the scans had revealed an interruption of the normal flow of cerebrospinal fluid, which indicated that Gregory was suffering from hydrocephalus.

As she encountered the blank faces of Ross and his parents as she discussed this, she gently went over what she had said, and then attempted to explain in as clear a way as possible what cerebrospinal fluid is and its function.

She told them how cerebrospinal fluid is formed in the brain and that it circulates through the brain and the space that envelops both the brain and the spinal cord. She informed them that there were signs of raised intracranial pressure in Gregory's brain because of the hydrocephalus.

To correct this, Gregory would need a further operation, to insert a shunt, to ensure a free flow of cerebrospinal fluid.

She tried to explain what a shunt was, variously describing it as a catheter, or a tube, which would aid the free flow of the fluid, but the idea of this was so alien to Ross that he now desperately blurted out,

'And where will the fluid drain away to?'

He had heard what Miss Bannister had said, but could not really comprehend it. The image sprang into his mind of a tube of some sort coming out of the side of Gregory's head constantly draining off fluid.

Sighing heavily, he told her that he didn't properly understand everything she was saying, and asked what Gregory's prognosis was.

She listened intently to this question and reflected before she spoke. Gently she broke to them the news that Gregory had severe spina bifida, that there would undoubtedly be paralysis, probably incontinence and brain damage, but tried to soften the blow by adding that the *complete* extent of his problems was only something that could be accurately assessed with time. The first step was to get him breathing. She explained that she felt that it could be the intracranial pressure which was responsible for his breathing problems and that the insertion of a shunt might aid the flow of the cerebrospinal fluid, which might enable him to breathe independently.

Ross was devastated at the thought of his newborn son having to undergo two operations and the pain that this might entail. He asked her then, 'And what if we just leave him alone?'

Miss Bannister thought for several minutes before answering this question. When she did so, she answered gently, telling him that it was difficult to reply to this, and that the only comment she could make was, 'Don't you think that perhaps Gregory should be given every chance?'

She asked then whether they would all like to see Gregory and she led them to the room he was in. This was an intensive care room, opposite the waiting room they had been in.

Ross's mum was to tell me later that she had despaired when given the news about Gregory, but had felt heartened that he was in the hands of a doctor who seemed both competent and compassionate. Furthermore, she didn't just encourage Ross to see Gregory, but also urged his parents to as well. The maxim of the hospital is 'Caring and Curing,' always written in that order, and over the following days not only me and Ross were to experience a high level of care during our stay there, but our families were too.

What Ross's parents' thoughts were as they

entered intensive care can only be imagined. Ross's mum told me that she had felt very frightened and that she had had to steel herself to enter the room.

What she saw was a shock to her. They saw a baby, who despite the fact that he was attached to various wires, tubes and machines, was so beautiful that he took their breath away. He wasn't simply a normal baby, but was truly beautiful. Having been born by caesarean he was not wrinkled, squashed, or blemished in any immediately visible way, but was an astoundingly *beautiful* baby. It may be that they expected to see a baby who looked as deformed as his condition was serious, but he was not.

Nature had smote her blow early in his development, in the early weeks of his formation, wreaking havoc whilst he was only a series of cells, a sheet of nerve cells which should curl at the edges and fold into a tube – called the neural tube – the normal closure of which encourages the formation of the spine and the covering of this with skin. This closure had not occurred. As limb buds had formed, and as Gregory had grown it was almost as though nature had compensated for the damage inflicted by imbuing him with a beauty which was breathtaking.

Ross's mum squeezed his arm tight as he looked at his son, a mix of pride and extreme sadness constricting his chest, rising up to his throat as though to choke him, and it was then that his mum told him that he would have to take one day at a time and try not to dwell on what might happen.

All Ross's dad could do was shake his head sadly and repeat over and over just how beautiful Gregory was.

Staff tended to Gregory caringly but unobtrusively throughout the visit, and at one point Ross saw movement in one of Gregory's legs.

'He can't be paralysed,' Ross exclaimed with some excitement.

A nurse gently explained that the movement was probably just a reflex action, but that time would reveal a more accurate picture of Gregory's condition.

Before leaving, Ross was informed that the operations were to take place that evening.

As they drove away from the hospital his parents bombarded him with more questions, and with a start of guilt his attention was diverted back to me. He wondered what was happening to me and whether my parents had been informed of the situation. Feeling that he couldn't just telephone them to ask, he asked that his parents drive him to my parents' house before he returned to Macclesfield to see how I was.

The roads were busy with commuters now making their way home from work and a silence fell in the car, each occupant lost in their own desperate thoughts. When they finally arrived at my parents' house in Marple his parents wanted to go in with him to talk to my parents.

Not knowing whether my parents knew anything of what had happened, Ross decided that he should talk to them alone. As his parents drove away he stood at the end of the drive feeling sick to his toes.

Taking several deep breaths, he approached the door on trembling legs.

Immediately upon seeing my parents he realised that they knew nothing about what had happened.

They listened in silence as he recounted as much as he felt able of the situation. Dad made him a cup of tea and they then put on their coats to accompany him to Macclesfield hospital to see me.

Dad drove calmly and quietly. Few words were exchanged on the journey.

... The Longest Night of my Life

It was early evening when they entered the ward. Ross sunk heavily into a chair alongside my bed, with my parents hovering at the foot of it. I was so desperate for news that I now fired question upon question at him with complete disregard for how tired and upset he looked. I was desperate to know what had happened. No staff appeared to bring more chairs so my parents stood helplessly and awkwardly as Ross tried to explain the events of the day.

Visiting time was over and it was so quiet on the ward that you could hear a pin drop and I knew that the other patients could hear our conversation. Feeling that the only way we could obtain any sort of privacy my father pulled the curtains closed around the bed.

Ross recounted what had happened at Booth Hall, and what Miss Bannister had explained about Gregory's problems, but as he was at a loss to understand what hydrocephalus was himself, he was unable to explain this aspect of the situation. He told me that Gregory was to have his two operations that night and that staff from Booth Hall would telephone him at home to let him know how these had gone.

As he disappeared to talk to the staff at Macclesfield, about getting me transferred to be with Gregory, my parents lingered by the side of my bed, not knowing what to say.

As he reappeared to tell me that the staff were going to try to organise my transfer for the following morning, he blurted out through a haze of tears and despair,

'You should see him, Fran, he is gorgeous.'

I felt overcome by bitterness that I had been separated from my baby in this way. As there was nothing anyone could do now but wait for news, my parents took Ross home, and again I was left alone with my thoughts.

Shortly a nurse approached to remove my drip. Once she had done this another nurse joined her to help get me out of bed. They told me that if there was to be any chance of me being transferred the following day that I would have to prove that I was fit enough for this. It was decided that I should walk down the ward to the bathroom at the end, with one nurse supporting me by the elbow and the other would walk on my other side carrying the bag of urine as I was still attached to a catheter.

At first they attempted to gently coax me to walk, but even this made me feel bitter. Although it was very painful to walk after the caesarean, with each feeble step I took on trembling legs I knew in my heart that this was going to be an act that Gregory would never be able to make.

Progress was slow and the ward was silent now. The nurses no longer spoke and I felt the eyes of each of the other patients watching my progress. I felt that the ante natal patients watched with a mix of pity and fear; possibly worrying about their own imminent births. I felt angry that I should be on this mixed ward as I am sure the sight of me could only have had the effect of making them feel very frightened.

When I finally reached the bathroom one of the nurses disappeared to complete other nursing duties, leaving me alone now with the nurse who was holding the bag of urine. She asked me whether I wanted to wash my face, tidy my hair and brush my teeth.

'Of course I do,' I replied heavily.

I asked her then to leave me in private, but she told me that she could not as I might faint or collapse and that it was not 'safe' to leave me alone. As she said the word '*safe*' all the anger which I felt about how events had unfolded since entering the hospital emerged.

Without regard for her as a person, or the fact that she was a nurse who had only just come on duty, and had not been involved in any previous incidents, I took the bag of urine from her and pushed her towards the door. As I hooked the bag onto a radiator I noticed her look of incredulity and a look of fear; probably because she knew that leaving me alone would be against hospital rules.

She pleaded with me now, imploring that she would be going against hospital policy if she didn't remain in the bathroom with me. I did not reply to her plea, but stared at her in a hostile manner. She edged her way backwards.

'Look I will get you a chair,' she told me, 'and you must leave the door ajar and call me if you need anything as I will just be on the other side of the door,' she told me.

She quickly brought a chair, but I remained standing. I stood impassive in the hospital bathroom, wondering just how events had brought me to this situation. I heard her shuffling on the other side of the doorway and I clutched the wash basin as wave upon wave of nausea and despair now swept over me. I splashed some water on to my face and then brushed my teeth, but this only served to make me retch.

I stared then at my reflection in the mirror above the basin but did not recognise the image which was reflected back at me. Not only did I look dishevelled and wild, but I was unrecognisable to myself. I felt a changed person in that instant and wondered how I could have bullied the nurse in such a way as I was usually a quiet, even timid, person.

I knew that the person who was going to leave this hospital would not be the person who had entered it. I knew that from now on I would be forever *changed.*

I unhooked the bag of urine from the radiator and with a look of relief the nurse took this from me. I was relieved by this action as it felt inordinately heavy and my legs felt like lead. I made my way back to my bed with pains shooting through where I had been cut open. I became numb to the effect of these, feeling them, but not caring about the pain. It was as nothing compared to the pain I carried in my heart at the thought of having a son who might be forever confined to a wheelchair. I wished only that my stitches would burst at the same time as my heart burst open and that I could fall to the floor dead so that there would be an end to the nightmare.

But of course this didn't happen. Instead I was settled in bed. It wasn't long before Mrs N, the midwife who had tended to me in labour, appeared at the side of my bed. She was dressed in a black cape and a rush of cold air entered with her, as though she had just come on duty from outside.

She pulled up a chair and told me that on arriving for duty that she had been told that I had had a baby with spina bifida and that she had come to offer her condolences. I stared at her in stony silence as her eyes told me to acknowledge her. She picked up my hand which was resting heavily on the bedclothes, the expression on her face one of supplication, willing me to talk to her.

I could find no words to say to her.

When she next spoke her sympathy seemed to have a hollow ring to it and I turned away from her. Replacing my hand on the bedclothes she hurried away.

And then a terrible *anger* overwhelmed me.

Why hadn't she shown any compassion or professionalism the night before when I had so badly needed it?

By now she had disappeared as quickly as she had appeared and I was never to see her again. I have always felt that everything about her attitude seemed to indicate that she didn't really care; that she was preoccupied with issues of her own, and that in the performance of her work that she was just going through the motions.

I felt completely isolated despite the fact that there were other patients on the ward and a lot of coming and going. A tea trolley was brought in and left in the middle of the ward for the patients to help themselves. No-one offered me a cup of tea, and I watched as the lady in the bed opposite with the baby walked towards it, almost doubled up with pain, clutching her stomach.

I heard the teacup rattle in its saucer as she made her laborious way back up the ward. It was with some surprise that she settled the cup on my locker with trembling hands. She introduced herself and offered me the tea. I declined this as I was feeling nauseous but was pleased as she carefully and with difficulty sat down at the side of my bed.

She told me how sorry she was about Gregory's problems and how she could understand how upset I must be feeling and how it was appalling that this should be exposed for the entire ward to see. She had a gentle manner and I appreciated her courage in coming to talk to me and the kindness in which she spoke, as she told me a little about herself and her new baby. It was her second child, and was a girl. She squeezed my hand before making her way to her own bed to get some sleep, telling me to call out to her if I needed anything.

Hot tears coursed down my cheeks as for a moment I felt enveloped in the warmth of the kindness shown by this stranger.

As the other patients drifted off to sleep I was given a sleeping pill. Despite this I could not sleep, unable to stop worrying about what was happening to Gregory, and whether he was still alive even.

At last a nurse appeared at the side of my bed. She told me that Booth Hall hospital had been on the phone, and that Gregory's operations were over. I asked her how he was and she replied that he was 'stable' but on a ventilator. She then gave me a painkilling injection and told me to try to get some sleep. Shortly, another nurse approached with the same news which Ross had telephoned with and asked her to impart to me.

I lay propped up on my pillows, wide-eyed, terrified. Gregory was alive. He had had his operations, but what now? One thought after another raced through my head. It all seemed so unreal, so difficult to take in. Only twenty-four hours earlier I had been looking forward to meeting my baby, but now felt trapped in a nightmare.

I couldn't even move very much and felt pinned to the bed as one tormented thought chased another round and round in my head.

What had gone wrong?

Would Gregory be completely paralysed?

Did he have extensive brain damage?

Only twenty-four hours earlier I had been expecting to deliver a healthy baby. I had had my baby, but didn't even really know what he looked like, other than from the blurred image of the photograph I had been given and my memory of him when I had seen him - which seemed to be fading fast. I had thought that things would be so different and that I would by now be cradling my baby in my arms.

Instead, I had to rely on my brief memory of him, and I was already having to try to come to terms with his problems and thinking about what we might have to contend with. I thought that if he was disabled but didn't have brain damage, that although this would be the most bitter of blows, that we could cope with this.

The thought of him not only being paralysed, but also brain damaged, hit me with such force that I physically clutched at my throat, feeling so anxious that I couldn't breathe. I wanted to die then. My heart hammered inside my chest as I broke out in a cold sweat, gasping for breath.

Bloodied, torn, and clammy with cold sweat, I wondered what I had done to deserve this torment.

Suddenly, it was as though a dam burst inside me as I began to cry as I had never cried in my life before. At first there were no tears, only racking sobs coming from deep inside my stomach. It was a physical wrenching, which started in the pit of my stomach, travelling up to my throat, emerging as strange dry, rasping sounds. I began to cough and choke as tears then began to fall heavily, my whole body shaking from head to toe. I had never felt so tormented and frightened in my life.

A nurse hurried over.

'Oh dear, you are not feeling very good are you,' she exclaimed.

In an effort to calm me she told me that Booth Hall hospital had been on the phone again with an update on Gregory's progress.

'They have tried taking him off the ventilator, but have put him back on it as he didn't attempt to breathe,' she informed me.

'This is ... *good news*,' she said, the last words spoken falteringly, and emerging more quietly as she looked away from me.

I stared at her. I could not *understand* how she could think that it was good news that he couldn't breathe. The thought entered my head that she must be a very stupid woman to think this.

With a desperate shake of her head and a squeeze of my hand she walked away. As she disappeared I thought that if Gregory couldn't even breathe unaided, how could he live?

This was how I was to spend the remainder of the night, with one terrible thought following another.

Occasionally, I calmed down and in these moments all my instincts told me that I already *knew* what the *real* situation was. I had felt it immediately after his birth. I knew in my heart that he was desperately ill, and that he would probably die; but as I had no certainty, I just couldn't stop thinking about all the different scenarios there could be.

Exhausted and desperate, I wished that we could both just die together at that same moment.

The Agonising Wait for Our Reunion

It seemed like an eternity before the hospital began to come to life. Once all the other patients had used the bathroom, I was again helped to walk there. The ashen face of a stranger stared back at me from the mirror this morning.

Ross appeared early. He was with his parents, who had driven him to the hospital as he had been told that I would be transferred in an ambulance and that he would accompany me in this to Booth Hall Children's Hospital where we would be reunited with our son.

I was sitting in a chair by the bed when they entered and his parents appeared visibly shaken when they saw me. They spent only a couple of minutes with us before returning home. They appeared at that time older than I had previously thought them.

We settled to wait for the ambulance together, Ross going for a coffee as someone appeared to remove my catheter and the dressing over my wound. As they replaced the dressing they tried to make conversation about how neat the wound was, but I could not see it over my still distended stomach, nor did I want to. I wasn't interested.

When Ross reappeared I was given a pain killing injection to help me on the journey, my thigh now pitted with tiny punctures from all the injections I had been given.

We waited anxiously. I could not have been thinking rationally because each time someone entered the ward I expected that they were bringing news that Gregory had died. I did not vocalise these fears then, but Ross knew that whilst Gregory was on life support that this wouldn't happen; but he paced up and down the ward nonetheless, impatient for the ambulance to appear.

At intervals during the morning he kept disappearing to ask hospital staff when the ambulance would arrive. We had forgotten that there was an ambulance strike, but the staff assured him that one would appear imminently as our case had been conveyed to ambulance staff as being urgent and although they were working to rule, they were still covering emergencies.

As the ward bustled with activity, with all kinds of people entering and leaving, and cards and flowers appearing for the other patients I felt close to completely breaking down, despite the fact that Ross was now with me. With the appearance of these cards and flowers for the other patients there emerged another feeling inside me.

It was one of feeling a complete failure.

Previously, I hadn't thought of how *I* might have expected to receive such messages of congratulations for us on the birth of our baby, but my eyes now pricked with tears at this omission.

Quickly I chastised myself for feeling such self pity when Gregory was lying so far away, and so poorly.

I was to feel even more of a failure later when a social worker popped her head round the curtain - which Ross had pulled round the bed for privacy; to ask if there was anything she could do to help us. She withdrew hastily as Ross was very abrupt with her, honestly at a loss to know why we should be approached by a *social worker*. She thrust a piece of paper at him with her name scribbled on it, and a telephone contact number should we wish to speak to her in the future.

I could palpably sense his anger building as minute followed minute, and hour upon hour dragged; and still no ambulance appeared.

It was lunchtime when he told me that he was going to get a taxi home, to get our car and that he would then collect me and drive us to the hospital himself. The staff urged him not to do this as they were sure that an ambulance would appear soon, and that I would not be able to sit in an ordinary car because of the caesarean wound.

The injection I had been given that morning had started to wear off and I was becoming more and more aware of feeling not just uncomfortable, but of stabbing pains shooting though my stomach. Another pain which I could not then identify also gripped me. It was the air which had become trapped inside my stomach as I had been cut open and then stitched up which was causing the pain.

Lunch was brought but I felt too upset and in too much pain to eat anything. I suggested that Ross eat it instead, as there was no knowing when he would next be able to eat. He was stopped from doing this by one of the staff - as it was against hospital policy. The meal was taken away, and it is likely that as it was now cold and congealed that it would probably have been scraped into a bin.

The inflexibility of the regulations and rules in this situation on such an occasion struck me as being ridiculous.

I went into panic mode as Ross left me alone on the ward for a few minutes while he went in search of a sandwich.

Please, I whispered, to goodness knows who – I certainly wasn't thinking of any God at that time, despite my Roman Catholic upbringing – *please don't let Gregory die without me having seen him. Please let me spend some time with him.*

Ross quickly reappeared, and again asserted that he was going to fetch our car from home. I asked one of the staff if I could now discharge myself as I intended to go with him in our car to Booth Hall hospital despite their objections. We were both now desperate that Gregory should no longer languish alone without us.

One of the staff must have got a doctor to come because a young lady doctor appeared and told us that an ambulance was definitely now on its way. She busied herself then, slowly performing her work as though to distract us. She took my blood pressure and performed all the other tasks she needed to discharge me. Finally, after what seemed an age, she gave me another pain killing injection for the journey.

Shortly, we heard a commotion outside the ward. A heated exchange seemed to be taking place.

We heard a man's voice loudly and angrily

asserting that the transfer of a 'mother' to another hospital was not classed as an emergency '... *that they were working to rule,*' his voice growing fainter, as though he was disappearing into the distance.

Thinking that the ambulance men had left, I broke down sobbing. I think that one of the staff must have taken them to one side to have a word with them, because suddenly a stretcher on wheels and two ambulance men appeared at the side of my bed.

The older one uttered gently,

'Let's get you on to the stretcher love.'

'Can't I go in a chair?' I asked.

'No,' he replied, firmly, but kindly.

A young midwife - possibly a trainee - had been assigned to accompany us on the journey, and she hovered alongside as I was lifted onto the stretcher.

I don't recall feeling anything other than relief as I was taken out to the waiting ambulance. No-one appeared to say goodbye, although the lady in the bed opposite whispered '*good luck, I shall be thinking of you Francesca - and of Gregory*' - she added, as we passed her bed.

I was sorry to think that I had already forgotten her name.

A wall of cold air hit me as I was wheeled outside to the waiting ambulance. It had been stiflingly hot on the ward, and the contrast of the icy air at first took my breath away. My breath caught in my throat as an icy breeze whistled around my wound, so that it stung, feeling both cold and then as though red hot pins were being stuck into it, despite the fact that I was very well wrapped up in nightclothes and blankets.

One of the ambulance men told me that they were going to lift me on the count of three, so I clutched my wound and held my body rigid against the onslaught of pain I felt that I would feel. As I was elevated into the air, I looked up at a grey autumnal sky, dirty-coloured clouds scudding quickly across it. It looked as bleak and depressing as I felt, but as the stretcher was locked into place inside the ambulance, and one of the men went to close the back doors before taking his place in the driver's seat; I greedily gulped in this fresh air, now feeling claustrophobic imprisoned inside the ambulance.

The younger of the ambulance men had remained inside the ambulance with us to assist the midwife as the ambulance slowly crawled through the hospital grounds, jolting over sleeping policemen.

I sadly recalled the jolts and joy I had felt when I had been carrying Gregory.

I was constantly monitored through the journey and repeatedly asked whether I wanted anything. I was offered something through a face mask. I don't know whether it was gas and air or oxygen, but I declined. The only thing I wanted was to be at the hospital with Gregory. I clutched my wound throughout the journey, praying that my stitches would hold until I got to Booth Hall hospital, and that I would not be returned to Macclesfield.

I didn't speak to anyone on the journey, not

even to Ross, but kept my eyes averted to the window, where if I looked up I could get an overhead view of outside. Ross told me at various stages where we were, and pointed out at one place that we were at the end of the road on the A6 near Stockport where my brother – Gerard – then lived.

I thought of the irony; that I had given birth to Gregory on this brother's birthday, but I doubted that we would ever share any joy in this fact.

The journey seemed long and laborious; the midwife's chatter banal. Perhaps she was making an attempt to ease the tension which seemed to grip the air inside the ambulance; but I felt myself becoming more and more depressed, and also *angry* with her, feeling that she had no respect for the way I was feeling as she talked incessantly *at* the driver, at times trying to draw Ross into conversation.

I felt as though the ambulance driver himself seemed to become fed up with the stream of non-stop chatter emerging from this young woman's mouth, or perhaps he was simply tired of the situation. Whatever he was feeling, he sighed heavily. This seemed to spur the midwife in a new direction and she now seemed to have become so bored that she attempted to begin to flirt with the young ambulance man. Eventually, he asked the driver to stop, and he went to sit up front alongside him, leaving me now in the care of the midwife, although he looked back to check that everything was alright every few minutes.

The midwife now lapsed into a strained

silence.

We were probably all then thinking the same thing, wishing for the journey to be over as quickly as possible.

I became aware that we were in the city when I noticed from the overhead view I had, fly posters stuck up everywhere, new ones pasted over the scraps of old ones flapping in the breeze, and lots of graffiti adorning the buildings. I recognised some of the sights of Manchester, recognising the Sunday Express newspaper building as it loomed into view. I stared at the large and impressive building constructed of shiny black glass, just able to make out through the opaqueness of the glass the shapes of huge printing presses within.

As we approached an area of Manchester hitherto unknown to me I felt a frisson of fear run through me. I could also sense Ross's apprehension as I realised that we were nearing our destination, and that we would imminently be reunited with our son.

Getting to Know Gregory

Neither of us voiced our fears as we approached the hospital. Although we had both been impatient to the point of anger when waiting for the ambulance to take us to Booth Hall, as we finally arrived at the hospital, a myriad of thoughts now entered our heads.

The overwhelming feeling *I* had was one of fear.

What awaited us inside the hospital?

I was not only afraid of seeing Gregory now – fearing that his head would be a mass of stitches and that we would be greeted by a tiny face contorted by pain; but I was afraid of the other patients too, expecting to see children who had been ravaged by the effects of treatment for cancer, and accident and burns victims.

I shook from head to toe as my stretcher was lifted from the ambulance. This time we entered through a different entrance, not the main entrance which Ross had used the day before.

I was wheeled down a corridor, which looked newly built and smelt of fresh paint, the lights overhead blinding me for a moment after the dull grey of the late afternoon sky. There settled in my stomach a feeling of sheer terror as we headed for ward 14 – the neurological ward where Gregory was being nursed.

Suddenly, another fear made me shudder. It was as though an icy finger of death touched my heart. All my senses became heightened then. Along with the smell of the paint I could now smell the usual scents familiar to many hospitals, that strange odour, which can only be described as seeming to consist of a mix of disinfectant and stale cabbage.

Something else also now assaulted my heightened senses. There seemed to me a smell of fear and sadness within the hospital. I could hear the heavy footsteps of the midwife and Ross walking behind the stretcher seeming to reverberate and bounce from the walls.

Then we were on the ward.

As if to confirm all my worse fears, the first sight which greeted me was that of a young patient in a wheelchair. Her body was small and deformed, her head large and misshapen. She smiled at me, but I could not meet her eyes. One word screamed inside my head – and that was *Gregory!* It is impossible to articulate the pain I felt at that moment.

I noticed that Ross's face was deathly white as we were shown into a side room at the top of the ward. He was later to tell me that from his standing position that he had had an overview of the ward, and that its patients had deeply shocked him. He said that it was the closest image of what it might be like to see the inhabitants of Austwich, or some other prison-of-war camp. Instead of seeing adults, whose bodies had been ravaged by starvation, disease and torture; what he saw were children, victims of another fate: either of accidents, violence, or the cruel vicissitudes of nature.

I was lifted from the stretcher on to a low bed with a duvet on it with a child's quilt cover with a picture of a BMX bicycle on it. A nurse introduced herself to us – I think that she may have said that she was called Alison, but I cannot accurately remember, even though we were to spend much of our time in her company over the next few days as she was involved in the intensive nursing of Gregory throughout his time at the hospital.

As the young midwife who had accompanied us on the journey shoved her notes into the hands of this nurse, a young boy strolled into the room through the open door.

'Hello,' he called in a cheery voice. 'I'm Roy.'

Another nurse came in and gently shooed him out. I was relieved to see that he was quite an ordinary boy with a cheery smile, the only sign of any injury being a mass of stitches on one side of his half-shaven head. The hair on the part which wasn't shaved flapped absurdly as he was ushered out of the room, but not before his mouth had broken into a massive grin, which lit up the whole of his face.

My heart stopped racing so fast then, and I felt ashamed that I hadn't even been able to manage a feeble smile at the young girl in the wheelchair.

I didn't have time to think anything more as a nurse appeared with a wheelchair which Ross assisted her to lift me into. I was wheeled into a room directly opposite the one we had been taken to. This was intensive care.

Immediately upon entering, my heart seemed to lurch inside my chest as I saw Gregory on a ventilator on the right hand side of the room.

Although only a tiny baby attached to various tubes and monitors, his body supported by a large roll of cotton wool; his *presence* seemed enormous and to dominate the room.

Two nurses tended to him as he lay half on his side, half on his back, with a huge bandage around his head. This bandage seemed to secure a series of tubes, one leading to his nose, and on closer observation he seemed to be wired up all over his body, the tubes and wires leading to large pieces of equipment surrounding the table he was on.

A name tag around his ankle read, 'Gregory Neild-Fielding,' and I felt upset that they had mistakenly transposed the letters *e* and *i* in my name. I felt a burst of pride that this was my baby and wanted his name to be spelt correctly.

As I was wheeled closer to him I could see the shape of his shoulders, arms and legs, beautifully formed, the silky smooth skin crying out to be touched; his shoulders a mini replica of the shape of Ross's.

Several adjustments were made to the site of some of the monitors and machines so that I could be wheeled as close as possible to him. His eyes were closed, tiny red lips slightly apart, revealing the inside of his mouth, whose moist flesh looked sweetly pink.

With quivering fingers I reached out to touch him. My fingertips throbbed with warmth, and I felt almost as though an electric shock passed through my whole body as I made contact with him. The contact was bitter sweet in its impact, bringing a lump to my throat so overwhelming that it now emerged as a strange strangulated sob.

I touched his legs, looked at his toes, and ran a finger down one arm, chubby almost, certainly not thin. When I reached his clenched fist I prised the balled fist open and placed my finger inside.

There was no response.

I became oblivious to anything else. The only life in the room seemed to be my own heartbeat, which seemed to fall into time with the pulse of his body.

I noticed how long his fingernails were. This had the effect of causing a large surge of anger to course through my body. I could not believe that nature could have created such a beautiful baby, down to the very tips of his fingernails, but at the same time wreak such damage in his development.

I was overcome by sadness and disbelief.

I felt enormous pain, mixed with immense pride, at the sight of this baby, who I had nurtured for nine months, and who I now *recognised* as being my son.

Nonetheless, it was strange too. Although Ross and I had both talked to and been involved with him for the previous nine months when I had been carrying him, now that he had been born he had become *known* in a way that we hadn't known the baby I was carrying.

He had become our son, a fully-fledged member of our family, not just a prospective member, whose sex we hadn't even known.

This knowledge served to compound the blow we both felt about how ill he was. I studied him for some sign that he knew that we were

109

now with him. There was none. I wondered at the extent of his difficulties. As a baby he looked like any other, but what would he have to contend with if he should live.

Was he suffering?

Would he start to respond more over the following days, and if he did, would we bond as I had not been with him in those crucial hours following birth?

If he did die, how would he die?

How could we cope with him dying?

Would he survive just to endure a lifetime of suffering?

As all these thoughts raced through my mind, l felt wave upon wave of sadness and nausea begin to overwhelm me.

Why had everything turned out this way?

As Ross pushed the wheelchair out into the corridor I began to sob bitterly.

The nurse assisted in returning me to the room opposite intensive care. She urged that I should be put to bed to rest. As I tried with her and Ross's help to get on to the very low bed I found that I couldn't make the movement to get down to the bed, having previously been in a high bed at Macclesfield that I had been able to ease myself on to.

The nurse said that she would try to change the bed for a higher one, and asked if Ross wanted her to try to obtain a camp bed for him to spend the night with me.

I was upset and surprised when he angrily retorted,

'No, and don't bother getting a higher bed. I am not staying here, and nor is Fran. We will go home and come back tomorrow. This is a terrible place.'

He told me that he definitely intended to go home now and get the car and return to the hospital to take me home.

'I don't like it here,' he added bluntly.

I shall never forget the nurse's response, or the calm and quiet way in which she responded saying,

'Do you not.' The words stuck in my mind as I had expected that she might have replied,

'Don't you?'

'No, I don't.' Ross replied abruptly.

The nurse remained very calm and told us that she would get the bed changed as quickly as possible, and that if we could both make ourselves feel more comfortable that this might make us feel a little better.

The nurse was non-judgmental and never passed any further comment about Ross's outburst, but Ross was to feel very guilty about this over the following days as she and all the nursing staff was kindness itself and could not have done more to help, not only Gregory but us as well.

While she was changing the bed for a higher one, Ross and I stood outside the room. At the top of the ward was a board with photographs pinned to it of the different ward staff. Further along the ward was another board. This one had scores of childrens' photographs on it, photographs of children of all ages, and with various ailments or problems.

'It's like a house of horrors,' Ross shuddered.

He had vocalised the feeling that I was

experiencing. Instead of seeing children, we saw, what at that time I am ashamed to say looked like monsters of various types. Instead of simply seeing children with a variety of illnesses and disabilities, but children nonetheless, whose parents could probably see beyond the physical, *we* saw only horror and deformity.

I was angrier than I had ever felt before. It was a vile, spitting, deep anger. My son did not belong here.

And then another thought struck me.

I realised that this was just where he *did* belong; that although Gregory was a beautiful baby now, if he lived he would grow into just such a child as those on the notice board: that his physical problems would become more visible as he grew.

This realisation hit me in such a physical way that I might have actually been hit with a brick.

Ross asked me whether I wanted to stay. I didn't know what I wanted. I certainly didn't like the place any more than Ross but now that we were here and I had seen Gregory, I was sure that I couldn't leave him.

I had shared my husband's life for fourteen years and my son's for only nine months, but now I could not choose between them. I loathed and feared the hospital as much as he did, but I knew that I wouldn't leave Gregory alone there.

The nurse appeared to lead me back to the room, where we found a high bed awaiting me, with a camp bed propped against the wall. She assisted me in to bed and made me comfortable.

Ross became calmer then, and decided that

he would stay with me. He had reasoned that while Gregory was on life support that he wouldn't die and had thought that we could visit the hospital every day, but sleep at home. He was to feel very guilty about the scene he had made as over the next few days we found that many parents staying overnight with their children on the main ward were sleeping in chairs alongside their beds. Not only did we both have beds but we also had the privacy of a separate room, which we were to become very grateful for.

Other parents settled down for the night wherever they could find a square inch of space, some on camp beds or other equipment which they had brought in from home, some simply spent whole nights fully dressed in a chair alongside their child.

There was a room at the bottom of the ward crammed with parents' belongings, and a waiting room at the top where drinks could be made and food eaten, but most parents spent the majority of their time with their children on the ward, husbands alternating with wives, and vice versa, as one parent tended to the responsibilities at home or work, while the other stayed with the poorly child.

Our parents visited that night and we sat with them quietly in the waiting room, no-one really knowing what to say.

The night stretched interminably ahead and we both tossed and turned when we eventually retired to bed, unable to sleep. At intervals one or other of us would get up and go in to see Gregory.

Each time I saw him, I was astounded anew at his beauty. The nurses tending him did so with compassion and only ever took their eyes from him if someone entered the room. Although rationally I knew that they were doing a job and doing it well, emotionally I resented them as I felt that it should be me who was looking after my son. I think that it was for this reason that I didn't make much effort to talk to them or learn their names, although I am sure that I was in such a state of shock and sadness that all my behaviour was at that time anything but normal.

At one point when Ross and I were in the room together and one of the nurses was changing Gregory's nappy she suggested that we should do this from the following day and also help to tend to his other needs.

She urged us both then to get some sleep as we looked exhausted and needed to build up some strength to help with Gregory's care. Before we left Ross asked what the different machines were for and this was explained to us. We were told that one machine was digitally recording the number of breaths per minute that it was providing for Gregory.

We returned to our room in silence, each preoccupied with our own individual thoughts.

As I lay in bed exhausted beyond being able to sleep I felt totally despondent about the whole situation. I felt that Gregory was not only not breathing for himself, but that he would *never* do so independently. I wondered whether Gregory could feel any pain or any sensation at all. It distressed me to see him lying there attached to so many machines and monitors, and I wondered whether it was futile to keep him artificially breathing. I thought of great aunt Bella's baby, who had been able to breathe, but had died approaching toddlerhood from meningitis.

As I thought of all that had happened, I shuddered, and thought that if it wasn't for all the machines Gregory would probably by now be dead. The thought seemed unbearable; but so was the situation he was in.

These thoughts raced round and round in my mind. There seemed to be no solution. I felt mentally tortured by the whole situation.

I couldn't bear to see him the way that he was, but I now couldn't bear the thought of him dying.

I felt then that it would have been better if he had died at birth before I had had the chance to get to know him, as my instincts had told me at Macclesfield.

The following day as we were encouraged to participate in his nursing I began to feel a *little* more optimistic. I noticed that his legs did move slightly from time to time, and I began to think that even if he was paralysed perhaps there was a chance that if he could start to breathe independently that he would live.

We spent most of the day with Gregory, our thoughts alternating between optimism and pessimism. All our emotions were very close to the surface, and on one occasion when Ross had been changing Gregory's nappy he angrily turned on one of the nurses and asked whether it really was necessary for Gregory to be attached to a rectal thermometer as well as all the other wires and tubes. He fastened Gregory's nappy without reinserting this, but the next time we changed his nappy it had been reinserted and Ross simply sighed heavily this time.

All through our stay at Booth Hall hospital we had visitors from both families, so although in one sense time dragged, we were so busy that we didn't seem to have a minute to spare. Every action I performed was painful and slow; the trek to the toilet seemed to take forever as this was situated at the bottom of the ward. Ross accompanied me as I couldn't manage this alone.

It was distressing walking down the ward as we saw the rows of beds with some very sick looking children in them. On our return from one of these trips the mother of a little boy at the top of the ward approached us to speak to us.

Her son had been involved in a car accident and had been in a coma since then. She had tears in her eyes as she told us that he didn't seem to be getting any better and that he just seemed to be a lifeless body now that she feared would simply fade away before her eyes. She seemed desperate to talk and I felt guilty as we hurried off back to intensive care to be with our son, unable to offer her any comfort.

That evening her husband came in to take her place. I was to become haunted by the face of this man, as each time he came in to be with his son he sat at the side of the bed like a robot; his face pale as a ghost's looking transfixed with pain and sadness with eyes only for his son. I never throughout the whole of our stay at the hospital saw this man speak to anyone as he kept his lonely vigil at the bedside of his child.

The expression on his face is etched on my memory.

In the privacy of our room we discussed our various thoughts about Gregory. At other times we were silent for long stretches of time, each preoccupied with our own thoughts about the situation.

Late that night as Ross dozed fitfully on the camp bed I again went in to see Gregory. I had been lying in bed having very dark thoughts, and I sobbed as I entered the room. One of the nurses looked up and asked me whether I had been intending to bottle or breast feed Gregory. I replied that I had been intending to breast feed but that this seemed irrelevant now.

She replied that I could if I liked try to express some colostrum and that they could give this to Gregory through a tube. In this way I could do something positive for him.

I didn't have the heart to tell her that it seemed pointless to do this under the circumstances as she seemed so keen to involve us in Gregory's care, so I told her that I would try this, and we agreed that staff would try to obtain a breast pump so that I could begin to do this the following day.

As I left the room I felt that everything was so wrong.

Things should not have turned out this way. I also felt upset, thinking that if Gregory had formed an attachment to anyone it wouldn't be *me*, that if he had bonded with anyone in those first few days of his life that it would be with one of the nurses who had constantly cared for him.

With a heavy heart I returned to bed and stayed there until the hospital came to life the following day. I dozed fitfully but I felt a heavy cloud hanging over me, my body startlingly jerking awake each time I dozed off. I didn't want to feed Gregory in this way. I didn't want to do anything anymore.

I wished that I could simply go to sleep and never wake up.

Instead, once more worries rushed in to my mind to torment me.

Was he going to live or die? my mind screamed in time with my thumping heart.

If he was going to die, I silently pleaded, *please let it be sooner rather than later.*

Please don't let him be paralysed and brain damaged.

The uncertainty of the situation seemed unbearable.

Unable to sleep properly, I got up at six o'clock, and on entering intensive care was for a moment blinded by the bright light shining over Gregory – day and night. When my eyes had had time to adjust, I noticed that Ross was already in the room being shown by one of the nurses how to wash Gregory's eyes with dampened balls of cotton wool, a separate one for each eye to prevent any possibility of cross infection.

I was tired, uncomfortable and in pain, and I sobbed at the sight of the two of them together tending to our son. I was angry that I had carried him for nine months, but that instead of me now caring for him he seemed to have become public property. Ross put his arm round me, and I noticed that silent tears were running down his face.

I don't think that we ever spent time with Gregory without crying at the pitiful situation he was in. Sometimes it was just silent tears, at other times strangulated sobs. At times we were overcome by uncontrollable racking painful cries, faces dripping with tears, saliva and running noses.

I have never felt so vulnerable and exposed.

That day we began to take some photographs of Gregory. As Ross worked for Ilford at that time, a company which specialised in producing black and white film, he had loaded his camera with this. We were long into the future to be grateful for these photographs, which have survived the ravages of time intact.

One machine had now become for us the predominant piece of equipment in the room, and that was the one which was recording how many breaths per minute Gregory was being given. It was with heavy hearts that each time we visited him we found that the machine was constantly controlling all Gregory's breathing; feeling that this didn't bode well for him ever breathing independently.

We returned to our room together despondent. There was breakfast awaiting me on a tray. Ross decided then that he would go in search of some breakfast and fresh air, but I urged him to eat what had been left for me as I had no appetite.

He told me that he needed some fresh air anyway, and disappeared from the room. I wanted to beg him not to leave me alone, not even for a few minutes. I knew that the fear I was experiencing was irrational but could do nothing about it. My heart thumped, my hands grew clammy and I felt a cold weight descend in my stomach. My legs were like lead.

Feeling overwhelmed by the claustrophobic nature the room had now taken on, I opened the curtains to be met with a lifeless dull grey sky. I felt like a prisoner then, trapped in the hospital, and felt that this could be how I might have to live in the future – in a hospital permanently at the side of my sick child. I felt as though I was going to die from sheer terror.

Looking out of the window at the quadrangle below did nothing to alleviate this fear. I stared at, without really seeing, a grassed area in the centre with childrens' play equipment, perhaps swings and a slide. I couldn't be sure as my vision had become blinded by fear. There sprang into my consciousness now the thought that I might never see Gregory play on such equipment as a child. I felt rooted to the spot, arms encircling myself as though I might shatter into pieces if I didn't hold myself tightly.

I was still in this position when Ross reappeared and chastised me for not eating breakfast. He told me that he had been talking to the mother of the boy in a coma and she had told him that there was a bathroom that the parents could use at the bottom of the ward. Ross told me that he would assist me there to take a shower.

As we made our way to the bathroom this

lady approached me and asked whether Gregory was any better. I could only shake my head sadly, unable to find any words to speak to her. She squeezed my hand and told me where her toilet bag was, and that I should use any of her toiletries that I might need.

We entered the bathroom through a chaos of parents' belongings and I realised that we were lucky to have a separate room to ourselves. Knowing that I would be unable to get into a bath, although I don't recall whether the room had one, it was decided that I should take a shower.

As I tried to make the step up into the shower cubicle I found that it was too painful. I felt overcome by despair and depression, and now didn't even have the energy or inclination to even want to wash.

Ross took over then, tenderly washing me from head to toe coaxing me as he did so as though I was a child. I was surprised by his gentleness and cajoling. Although we had always experienced an intimate and fulfilling sexual and emotional relationship I now saw a side of him that I had never before seen. The experience although in actuality very intimate and physical became one of sheer emotion. It felt asexual but meaningful. As he helped me change the heavy pad soiled with lochia I realised that whatever the future should bring for both of us that we would in some way be forever bound together by this experience.

It wasn't one either of us would have wished for but it was unique to us and we would forever share it.

As Ross showered, I made my way back up the ward slowly. Again the mother of the boy in a coma approached to speak to me. She was dark haired and very pretty but her face contorted as though she had slipped on an ugly mask as she spoke of the bitterness she was feeling towards the driver who had knocked her son down. I understood the bitterness she was feeling as my thoughts had now started to reflect on my pregnancy and labour and how events had evolved to lead us into this situation.

Later that morning as I watched Ross leaning over Gregory, his hand cupped around the top of one of his legs, silent tears trickling down his cheeks I felt angry, not only at seeing my son in the situation he was in, but also at the pain which was registered on my husband's face. I felt then that it would have been better had Gregory's problems been spotted early in the pregnancy and I had had a termination. Then I was overcome by guilt at this thought.

How could I possibly even think such a thing?

I became blinded by tears at the thought of destroying my own beautiful baby, who now lying so helplessly before my very eyes.

In an effort to cheer us up, one of the nurses showed us something else that we could do for Gregory. We could help to keep his mouth and lips moist. This was done by the insertion into his mouth of a long stick with a moistened pad on the end of it. As she placed this in Gregory's mouth his lips did seem to close slightly around it, and I wondered whether this was a reflex action, a baby's mouth in search of a nipple, but couldn't be sure that his mouth was actually moving, feeling that I was willing it to do so.

Later, a midwife appeared to see me from outside. I felt weary and depressed as she went through the rituals of her job. Perched at the edge of the bed I stared silently and rudely as she sat opposite me on the bunk bed, skirt riding up over fat knees revealing flabby thighs. She prattled on oblivious it seemed to what I was feeling.

Suddenly, she pulled a breast pump from her bag, deciding that she was going to show me how it worked. As she lunged towards me with this, it seemed such an offensive weapon that she might have been brandishing a gun as far as I was concerned.

As she came towards me, nails bitten to the quick, I was about to physically push her away as Ross entered the room. Quickly assessing the situation he asked her to explain to him how it worked as I was feeling very tired and that we would try to use this later.

She seemed happy to lecture at length on this and I was now so angry feeling that she was so out of touch with how we were feeling that I just wanted to tell her to *piss off*. She left as she had entered, clumsily and loudly.

I was startled by the depths of my anger towards her as she disappeared back to the outside world from where she had come.

Ross disappeared, I think to get the breast pump sterilised.

I lay on the bed motionless, suddenly devoid of emotion. I had experienced so many extreme emotions one following so quickly on from another that I now felt completely numb.

Later Ross asked whether I was going to try the pump. I stared at him vacantly.

'I can't do it,' I responded.

'Just try,' he urged gently. 'Just give it a go for Gregory. You said you were going to breast feed the baby.'

'It shouldn't be like this,' I wailed.

'No, it shouldn't,' he replied in such a hurt way that I decided for his sake that I should try with him relaying the instructions he had been given by the midwife on how to use it.

My heart wasn't in the task and it seemed a waste of time as I had no breast milk yet. Eventually between us we managed to squeeze a few droplets of colostrum from each nipple.

As Ross went to deliver this to the nurses to give to Gregory it was greeted with as much celebration as if it was gold or some other precious entity. Every time I used the pump I felt very despondent about using it, thinking that everything felt so wrong.

Shortly it was decided that it would be good for me to leave the ward for a while. I was still finding it difficult to walk so a wheelchair was produced for me so that Ross could push me to the canteen. Each time I used a wheelchair I reflected on the possibility of Gregory being permanently confined to one.

I began to panic as I was pushed from the ward. Although I had felt like a prisoner when on the ward, now that I was moving away from Gregory I felt profound fear. I *couldn't* leave him. I *shouldn't* leave him, were the thoughts I now experienced.

I could sense Ross's relief as we travelled along the corridor. It felt vast and cold after the warmth of the ward, and I shivered despite the fact that I was covered in a blanket. Although I had found the ward claustrophobic I felt frightened of being away from it now. Although we had only been there for a couple of days it seemed as though we had been there forever and that was where we now *belonged*. During our time at Booth Hall hospital time seemed to pass in slow motion.

It was as though time had lost all meaning since entering the hospital.

As each step took us further away from Gregory I felt more and more pains shooting through my stomach which felt strangely empty and odd. The corridors were almost deserted, and I was glad of this as the people we did encounter stared for a moment at the sight of us, not used to seeing an adult in nightclothes in a wheelchair in a children's hospital.

As the canteen wasn't open we bought some sandwiches from a snack bar manned by middle-aged ladies probably working on a voluntary basis. I couldn't eat the sandwiches as my mouth felt so dry, and although I hadn't eaten now for almost four days I wasn't hungry.

'What's going to happen, Ross?' I asked.

'I don't know,' came back his weary reply.

It was then that I noticed that his hair had become flecked with grey, and that deep lines had appeared etched into the skin around his eyes. His mouth was set in an expression which I hadn't seen before; an expression I was to become familiar with over the following months. It would be a long time before I was to see him laugh again, even longer before his laughter or smile was to light up his eyes as it had so easily in the past.

The arrival at the hospital of Ross's twin brother, Lee, who had travelled from Scotland, lifted his spirits a little. His arrival for Ross heralded a semblance of normality as Lee seemed to bring into the hospital with him something of the outside world. It seemed to ease some of the tension in Ross, making the situation seem less intense.

As Ross explained to his brother how trapped he felt at the hospital Lee offered to drive him to our house so that he could collect the car so that he would be able to come and go as he wished.

As they left the ward to do this I felt *terrified*. I wanted to throw myself at Ross's legs, to clutch at them to prevent him from leaving me alone with Gregory. But I had too much pride to do this, and instead returned to our room where I wept copious tears.

I felt then that this was how the future would be, that Ross would still be able to go about his ordinary business but that my life now would be dominated by looking after a sick child. Then I couldn't even cry as I became rooted to the spot by fear at this thought.

Time seemed to stand still as I realised that my previous life was over. My eyes couldn't focus. I felt lost in space and time; as though being sucked into an enormous vacuum, whose size seemed to mock me as I felt as tiny and insignificant as a pin prick: understanding for the first time my importance in the scale of the universe. I wanted to cry out, but I had become mute. I wanted to feel arms encircle me to comfort me, but instead I was disappearing, being transported away from reality into a black hole. I seemed to be travelling through space and time, and felt that I was moving from life to death.

Just as I was sure that I was about to die, a voice pierced my consciousness, and hands gripped my shoulders.

'Oh Fran, *I am so sorry*. I shouldn't leave you alone. It was just that I felt so trapped, and wanted to get away from this place for a while.'

Ross had returned alone. He had got into the car with Lee, but on reflection and after chatting with him for a while, had decided that he should not leave me at the hospital alone. Lee had gone to stay at their parents' house, but had promised to return at any time he was needed, day or night.

It took a long time for me to recover my composure, and my whole body erupted in huge shuddering sobs. Although Ross had returned, there had now entered my consciousness the thought that our experience of this situation was going to be different, even though we were in it together now. As the mother of a disabled baby I felt that I would be called upon to bear the most physical responsibility - and it was a thought which I found overwhelming.

When I had sufficiently recovered, we went to intensive care together to see Gregory. Again his eyes were closed. Throughout the whole of the time that he was nursed there we never saw his eyes open, and this along with the fact that he wasn't breathing for himself upset us each time we saw him.

The nurses were, as usual, kind to us as we approached. At no time did they make us feel that we were in the way. This time one of them spoke directly to me. 'You haven't held Gregory yet, have you Fran.'

I replied that I had not.

The nurses pondered aloud on how this might be achieved. A chair was placed alongside the table, and it took what seemed like an eternity for the nurses to adjust all the monitors, wires and tubes to enable them to lift Gregory onto my lap without disturbing any of the equipment or wires he was attached to.

I became aware that I was trembling from head to toe as I waited to hold my baby for the first time since he had been born. One of the nurses gently lifted him as the other checked all his monitors, holding aloft some of the wires which were in the way.

As he was lowered carefully into my arms I noticed immediately that he was warm and soft, but it was so difficult to know how to hold him without disturbing the tubes or wires that I became frightened that one might become detached, or that I would drop him and that he would slip to the floor and be further injured.

Added to this, I became so overwhelmed by this first real contact with Gregory that my whole body racked with sobs. I was disappointed by this, feeling that it could only serve to distress Gregory, but I couldn't stop crying.

Although warm and soft, Gregory appeared

lifeless. He didn't look comfortable, but nor did his face register any pain.

I cried for him, and I cried for myself. I cried at my own shortcomings as a mother, at my own incapacity to find the strength and the courage through my cradling of him to convey to him love and security.

The nurses returned Gregory to the table, and I was left feeling hopeless and helpless and feeling that I hadn't helped Gregory at all. I wondered then if he should live what sort of mother I would make, thinking that he would have to live in an institution as I wouldn't be able to cope.

I wondered how in just a few days I had changed so much. I seemed to have changed from a generally intelligent and competent person into a jabbering wreck that couldn't stop crying.

I stumbled from intensive care with these disappointing thoughts. As we left we became aware of a terrible wailing. It was coming from the room next to ours which was opposite intensive care. Throughout our stay we had noticed this room, but had not known whether it was occupied as curtains had been drawn across the window facing the ward so that no-one could look in.

The noise now coming from within was a prolonged high-pitched mournful cry. It sounded half-human, half-animal. It was a terrible sound and Ross and I looked at each other in terror.

The curtains of the window overlooking the corridor were open now, and as we passed the room to return to our own we caught a glimpse of what was in there. We registered the pitiful sight of a small child who lay face down on the bed, a shock of red curly tousled hair not giving any indication as to its sex, and although its face was buried in the pillows this did nothing to muffle the terrible cries it was making.

The child lay immobile secured to a wooden contraption, the likes of which I had never seen before. Each of the child's legs was splinted and a thick wooden splint ran between the two so that the child's legs were forcibly kept wide apart.

A nurse was sitting alongside the child holding its hand trying to comfort it, and she waved as we passed. Perhaps she noticed our looks of terror and bewilderment because she now rushed out to speak to us.

She tried to reassure us that the child wasn't in pain, but was crying in frustration and anger.

'Don't get upset about it,' she urged us both, squeezing my arm before returning to tend to the crying child.

Ross and I exchanged looks of terror, not at all reassured by her explanation, wondering if we were to experience anything like this with Gregory in the future, but neither of us voicing the silent fear. Instead we simply clutched each other, the terrible wailing seeming to reverberate around the hospital and to echo in our minds long after it had stopped.

On our return to the room we both sat slumped on the bed in silence, thinking our own private thoughts, which I am sure could only have been equally dreadful.

Later that day, another boy was rushed into intensive care having been injured after running out in front of a car. We only had eyes for Gregory, although I was relieved that we couldn't see this little boy and consequently his injuries as a humidifier constantly pumped vapour around his bed to keep the air moist so he was concealed in a cloud of steam. I felt impassive now as I wondered how badly injured he was and whether he would die.

We were told by a doctor tending to this boy that Miss Bannister, the neurosurgeon, would be coming to visit us in the morning to talk about Gregory's condition.

Before retiring to bed that night we studied the photograph of her pinned to the notice board at the top of the ward. She looked a very ordinary woman on the photo but I urged Ross to tell me about her.

'Is she approachable?' I asked concerned about whether or not we would be able to communicate with her after my previous negative experiences with the doctors at Macclesfield.

'Yes,' he replied. 'She expressed herself in a way that I could understand when I met her,' he said, adding, 'and she listened carefully to what I had to say.'

As we lay on our separate beds reflecting on our own thoughts I wondered whether we were thinking the same thoughts, or whether our thoughts were as divided as the gulf between the beds.

I looked at Ross, and as he caught my eye, he said,

'Try to get some sleep. We will know more tomorrow after the doctor has been.'

It was impossible to sleep but it now became impossible for us to talk to each other. I think that we were both now frightened of the consequences of what tomorrow would bring.

Throughout the night my mind worked overtime imagining all the different scenarios there might be for us in the future.

The least distressing was that Gregory would be physically handicapped but not brain damaged. The thought of him being paralysed, brain damaged and incontinent sent a shudder of pain through my body. As I watched Ross dozing lightly now *his face etched with pain* I thought that if this was to be the case then I would break up our marriage and take over responsibility for Gregory's welfare myself. I had seen how trapped Ross had felt and reasoned that he had a whole life ahead of him and that with time and support from his brother, family and friends and interest in his work that *he* could at least live some semblance of a normal life.

However, I felt very despondent about the whole situation thinking that whatever Gregory's prognosis was it was a no-win one.

Wherever my thoughts took me, and from one minute to the next they envisaged every possible scenario, I was left feeling despondent.

And then a dreadful thought sprang into my mind.

There was a solution.

If Gregory was indeed paralysed, brain damaged and incontinent, if he was to live simply to exist without any quality of life, his existence being one of only pain and discomfort, then I could kill him. I could smothercate him and put him out of his misery.

As this thought entered my head, a dark cloud descended over me.

Would I do such a thing?

Could I do it?

And then bitterness swamped me. It was as though all the events of the previous days had accumulated, and now enveloped me in such darkness that I felt as though I was in hell itself.

I became overwhelmed with anger and sadness at how events had transpired. I thought of Gregory, who was either to die after only a few miserable days of pain and suffering, or to live afflicted by so many problems.

And then guilt kicked in.

A guilt which I knew I would have to live with for the rest of my life.

I wondered about just what kind of person could even think about killing their own child. Was I a monster? Or was I simply a mother pushed to the brink of despair?

I expected I could be regarded as both.

Perversely, now that I had faced all the different scenarios head on I felt strangely calmer.

It was as though I had cleared my mind so that I could now think with clarity.

Since Gregory's birth all my instincts had told me that Gregory would never breathe independently and that he was going to die, that in fact his body had been kept alive artificially, and that when treatment was stopped that he would in fact die.

I knew this without a shadow of doubt, but had been unable to stop the wheels of the machinery which operate medicine from setting in motion a chain of events which had only lead to pain and suffering; not only for Gregory, but for us too.

And tomorrow we would have the opportunity to discuss this with the consultant. As I lay in bed with a heavy heart, as the early hours of Saturday morning approached, I felt as I imagined a prisoner might feel awaiting execution on Death Row. It wasn't my death I awaited, but Gregory's.

I knew though that with Gregory's death there would die a fundamental part of me.

Hello Becomes Goodbye

I must have eventually dozed off, because I woke with a start with my heart thudding. I felt as though I had woken *from* a nightmare. Instead I had woken *to* a nightmare. It took a moment or two to remember where I was, and that the neurosurgeon would be talking to us today.

My body jerked uncontrollably as I recalled the events of the previous days. I felt sick with fear. Ross's bed was empty and I assumed that he was perhaps already with Gregory, the twisted sheets and blankets looking as though he had left hastily.

I pulled on my dressing gown and made my way as quickly as possible to intensive care. The little boy who had been there the day before had gone, and although I wondered whether he had died or been moved, I didn't care. My only concerns now were for *my* son.

Ross looked pale and drawn as he leaned over Gregory.

Later that morning, a middle-aged male doctor hurried in. He asked us whether we had cuddled Gregory and we replied that we had in so far as the constrictions of the life support machinery would allow us to. He looked at us pensively, making adjustments to various pieces of equipment, wires and tubes. Before he left he turned up the machine which was controlling Gregory's breathing - to the vocal consternation of one of the nurses tending to him - so that he should receive more breaths per minute than he had previously been receiving.

Ross's face spoke volumes as he excused himself. Alone in the room with the nurses, an eerie silence pervaded. We made no eye contact, all focusing on Gregory now.

The doctor had removed the bandage from around Gregory's head which had been securing the tubes to his nose and had replaced this with tape. As I stared at Gregory, eyes swimming with tears, I saw him as though through a mist, feeling extremely frightened.

As this eventually cleared, I saw him anew. I cried out then, a loud, terrible wail. His head seemed to have become elongated and misshapen. It may have previously been like this, but if it had, it had been hidden by the bandages.

I felt almost hysterical then, rushing from the room to find Ross. I could scarcely speak, I was so choked with fear, as I tried to tell him about Gregory's head.

We returned to the room together.

There we found Gregory wearing a bonnet. I sobbed then and asked the nurse whether Gregory's head had become misshapen. She did not reply, but I noticed that her eyes were swimming with tears.

Ross disappeared again to try to find out when Miss Bannister would be coming to see us.

I paced the corridor between our room and intensive care trying to calm the feelings of hysteria which were now threatening to overwhelm me.

A young doctor passed and went into

intensive care. I followed him in.

He stood poised over Gregory with a syringe about to take a sample of blood. I noticed that a bandage on Gregory's arm was beginning to look a little worse for wear, fraying at the edges.

And then I lost all control.

All the pent up emotions and anxieties from the previous days flooded over me. Suddenly I was screaming uncontrollably. Then I directed all these feelings at the doctor standing over Gregory, shouting at him, questioning what he was doing. I cornered him, so that he was pinned against a wall, with no place to escape to as he quietly said that he had been about to take a blood sample. His eyelids dropped to cover his eyes as he spoke, whereupon he then became stock still, staring sadly at the floor.

I felt sure in that instant that if he had tried to continue with his task that I would have punched him; and, indeed, that at that moment, had enough strength to break his jaw: and would have done so if he had attempted to continue.

Instead, his sad face tore at my insides.

I began to scream hysterically, crying aloud about just how much more suffering Gregory was to be put through; as one of the young nurses who had tended to Gregory during the whole time he had been nursed in intensive care ran from the room sobbing.

I became aware of lots of people running about, but I couldn't move. I had lost all control over myself, had lost all capacity to do anything other than to scream hysterically.

The nurse, who had run from the room -

and Ross, alerted by my screams, rushed back to me, and gently led me to a room at the top of the ward with the promise that Miss Bannister would join us shortly. As we entered this room I noticed a large number of staff assembled in the corridor as though about to perform a ward round.

Ross and I waited for Miss Bannister, both sobbing inconsolably now, with the young nurse kneeling beside my chair trying to comfort me. Another nurse brought in a tray of tea. She stroked my hand and urged me to have a sip of tea, but I didn't want it. Instead, I cried, as I had never cried before, unable to stop the flow of tears, saliva from my mouth, and snot running from my nose.

I knew that what was about to happen was going to be the most difficult thing I had ever had to do. I felt in those few minutes while we waited that it was now imperative at all costs to take Gregory off life support and let him try to breathe for himself; and that if he couldn't that he should be allowed to die in peace, and with whatever dignity was left to him.

I *knew* what the consequences of taking him off life support would be; and in one sense I felt that I would be *killing* him by doing this. However, all my instincts as a mother, and all my emotions as a human being, told me that it was inhumane to leave Gregory in the situation he was for a moment longer.

I not only felt frightened, but hated myself for wanting to take him off life support, feeling sure that this would result in his death, but I also felt sure that this was the right thing to do.

I silently cursed nature for having given me such a beautiful baby who I had grown to love so much, but who was so damaged.

With growing feelings of anger and despair, I noticed that the room was filling with people. Both the doctors who had visited Gregory earlier that morning, along with assorted nursing staff, crammed in.

Miss Bannister, the neurosurgeon, pulled up a chair alongside me, taking my hand. She held this in silence for several minutes as my whole body shook with anger and despair, my face wet with tears.

When she did finally speak, it was so quietly that she might have been talking to herself as she uttered,

'It is so cruel, so very, *very* cruel.'

I continued to sob inconsolably, tears and snot running from the end of my chin spilling onto my dressing gown.

'Why don't you kick off the conversation,' she gently urged.

In return for her kindness, I verbally attacked her, I was so overwhelmed with anger.

'You doctors, who do you *think* you are – *God?'*

This last word I spat out with all the anger which had been building up in me since my labour and Gregory's birth at Macclesfield hospital.

'Why are you putting my baby through more and *more* pain? If he can't breathe, and can only be kept alive by so many machines why don't you allow him to die in peace and with dignity?'

'What *right* do you have to determine what should happen to him, do you think that you are *Gods*,' I spat out the last word angrily again.

I heard the middle-aged male doctor let out a loud, sob and then he blew his nose noisily. The young nurse also sobbed, huge racking sobs.

Now that I had voiced the words which had been lying dormant in my mind – although they had been in my consciousness but had been *too terrible to voice,* I became calmer.

It was the doctors and nurses who were crying.

'Look at me,' Miss Bannister urged. 'We are not Gods and you are right to speak out. Doctors need to be *told*,' she continued as I *saw* her for the first time, having become dry-eyed but wild.

She was a very ordinary looking woman, wearing ordinary clothes beneath her white coat, and her face was kindly as she squeezed my hand and encouraged me to talk.

Then the words came tumbling out. I told her how painful it had been to see what our baby had been put through in the last few days, how it felt not to have held him, and how it felt to watch him in intensive care being kept alive by so many machines and monitors, attached to so many tubes and wires, not knowing whether he was suffering pain and discomfort. I voiced my fear that he didn't even *look* alive, that he wasn't moving and that I hadn't seen him open his eyes.

She listened carefully, pausing for a few minutes before she responded. She held my hand more tightly as she discussed Gregory's condition and prognosis. She told us gently that the part of Gregory's brain which controls breathing had not developed properly or was damaged. I couldn't take in what she was saying, and more tears fell onto my dressing gown as she went on to explain that they had performed the operation to insert a shunt to see if the shunt would relieve some of the pressure caused by the hydrocephalus, and allow him to breathe independently. The fact that he had not done so after the operation had not boded well; indicating that his brain was not properly developed, or was damaged, but that they had decided given the circumstances of how he had been transferred to them, to monitor him for a few days, to allow him every opportunity for any improvement, and for us to be involved with his care.

She told us that there had been no improvement.

She asked us then what *we* wanted to do.

I looked at Ross, as *I* told her that if that was the case that we wanted to take Gregory off life support and allow him to be cradled by us and that he should be allowed to die in peace and with some dignity. She turned to Ross then and he told her that this seemed to be the only option now, given the circumstances.

'Are you *both* quite sure of this she asked?'

We replied that we were.

'Do you *fully understand* the consequences of taking Gregory off life support,' she asked turning from me to Ross as we both replied that we did.

She responded that we had made a brave decision to take Gregory off life support, and asked *when* we would like to do this.

Ross answered,

'As quickly as possible: I don't think that he should suffer for a moment longer.'

Once again she asked us if we understood the *implications* of what we were about to do, and we again replied that we did. She went on to tell us that if we didn't feel up to doing it ourselves that we could go home and that staff would do this for us. She also offered us the opportunity of going home for the weekend, to return on Monday to remove Gregory from life support if we needed more time to discuss this and prepare for it.

We both replied that nothing else seemed right under the circumstances but to remove Gregory immediately from life support and let him die in peace with us.

She told us that staff would prepare Gregory and would bring him to our room to us, allocating a nurse to be at our disposal to help for as long as we needed her.

I felt sick with apprehension about what we were about to do. I had never seen a dead person, let alone someone die – and now I had to prepare myself to watch my first child die. This was the bitterest blow I could imagine.

Miss Bannister squeezed my hand and asked,

'And, what about *you*?'

I had no idea what she was talking about, so stared blankly back at her.

'She hasn't had a caesarean has she?' she asked one of the nurses, who replied that I had.

'Oh dear,' she responded, adding, 'In that

case I think that you should return to the maternity hospital. You need to look after yourself - your uterus – for your future childrens' sake.'

I replied angrily that I would not be returning to the maternity hospital, before adding very bitterly, *'and there will be no more children.'*

With a sigh, and a last squeeze of my hand, she left, followed by all the other staff, except the nurse who had been placed at our disposal.

She told us that it would take some time to remove Gregory from life support, but that as soon as he was ready she would bring him to our room. It was at this point that another nurse bobbed her head round the door to tell me that my father was on the phone.

I hurried off to speak to him, not wanting to waste a moment in returning to our room, and Ross hurried outside for a smoke. I hastily told my dad that I couldn't speak to him as Gregory was being prepared to die.

'I really don't know what I am supposed to do ... what formalities there will be,' I added, before saying goodbye and putting the receiver down.

I heard my dad take a sharp intake of breath, saying that he would come to the hospital to see if there was anything he could do.

I hurried back to our room and met Ross in the corridor.

'Am I *killing* our son?' I asked him.

'No,' he replied.

'*I* asked for him to be taken off life support though,' I responded.

'There isn't any alternative,' Ross replied. 'I think that Miss Bannister wanted to involve us in Gregory's care. There could not be any different outcome,' he added, sobbing bitterly.

As he entered the room ahead of me, his shoulders drooped in despair and his body shuddered with sobs. I didn't cry now. I *couldn't* cry. I felt beyond tears. I was numb with shock and despair. I felt at that moment that I would never experience any emotions ever again. I had used up all of them, and from now on there would be an empty vacuum where I had ever felt anything.

It was Saturday the 25th November 1989. As the nurse carried Gregory carefully into our room I felt the numbness I was experiencing at that moment would last a lifetime, that the experience we were about to go through would leave me so bereft of emotion that I would never feel *anything* again.

Of course it did not. After the initial numbness and shock of that day had diminished I experienced every emotion possible. Not a day has passed since when I haven't thought about Gregory, nor felt a void in my heart, a small empty space which can't be filled by anyone, or anything else.

I can say with all honesty that I have never come to terms with his death; nor after all this time expect to. I have learned to live with it. And over the years I have come to value my son's short life more than I would ever have thought possible. Although time has not healed the pain I feel - indeed every milestone which should have marked the progress of Gregory's life has perhaps been more intense than if he had lived: and I had watched him undertake it as a proud mother, or indeed experienced his suffering with him as the mother of a disabled child.

In intervening years I have written and thought about all the events leading up to, and surrounding his birth, and how I felt after his death, but it took many years to face up to the actual process of his death which I now describe.

I sat on the bed supported by pillows as the nurse handed Gregory to me. He seemed tiny and I felt awkward at first as I took him from her as he seemed so small and fragile. Where previously he had looked large when on life support wearing only a nappy, swamped in a blanket or shawl of some kind, and dressed in clothes which I didn't recognise, which swamped his tiny body, I realised how precious the little bundle I was holding was to me. A white bonnet covered his head, with the motif of a baby duck sewn onto the front.

I felt excited to finally be able to cuddle Gregory, but my heart pounded with dread at the thought that he was about to die. His body seemed warm and his tiny hands seemed to clutch at the blanket which covered him. My hands were sweaty; in fact perspiration seemed to seep from every pore of my body as I began to shake so uncontrollably I felt that I might drop Gregory.

His mouth stretched wide open as a shaft of sunlight from the weak November sun highlighted his beautiful face. His eyes flew open and I was startled to see how dark they were. I became aware of Ross at the side of the bed taking photographs. I felt greedy to maintain contact with Gregory but could sense the longing which Ross was feeling to hold his son.

I handed our son to him and Ross buried his face in his tiny body, sobbing uncontrollably. I picked up the camera, pointed it at the two of them and snapped father and son together. As Ross lowered Gregory to look at him Gregory's eyes fixed on Ross's face, their pupils enlarged.

I took Gregory then and it was as though some rational thought entered my consciousness as I began to notice his breathing.

Not knowing what to expect when they had brought Gregory in to us I became even more frightened at this point because Gregory was attempting to breathe. The thought entered my head that perhaps Gregory could survive independently, and that we had perhaps damaged him more by taking him off life support. My stomach felt so heavy and cold, it was as though there was a huge block of ice inside me.

We both watched terrified as he struggled to breathe. There was no regular pattern, but he was attempting to breathe, at first a shallow inhale, then a long pause, then his mouth gaped wide as he tried to take another breath, then he didn't breathe at all for a while; but a minute or two later would try again. A slither of vomit or saliva dribbled from his open mouth, and I wiped it away with my hand.

As the nurse popped her head round the door to see if we were alright, Ross told her excitedly that he was breathing.

'He is very grey,' she replied gently, before leaving us alone again.

Not only had the colour of his skin changed, but I now noticed that his tiny hands which I caressed felt colder now. I rubbed them, desperately trying to put some warmth back into them. I felt overwhelmed by helplessness as I noticed that his eyelids were almost closed now.

The last memory I have of Gregory alive is the distressed look on his face as I handed him to Ross for a final cuddle. Somehow – and at the best of times I cannot take photographs – I managed to snap the two of them together as Gregory died in Ross's arms.

As he handed him back to me I noticed that Ross was covered in a black sticky substance – meconium, which had escaped his nappy as Gregory's bowels had emptied as he had died. I sat on the bed numb with shock, holding Gregory without knowing what to do. I caressed his beautiful face, but he could have been a doll as he became limp, and I knew beyond doubt that he was definitely dead.

I lost all sense of time and feelings of emotion as the nurse and Ross eventually prised Gregory from my grip so that they could take him away to clean him.

I have no idea of how long they were gone, but I didn't move from the position I was in on the bed I felt so shocked. Eventually, he was replaced in my arms and a cot was set up alongside the bed so that we might lay him in this.

When my arms started to ache from his weight, Ross placed him gently in this cot. I noticed that he had cleaned himself.

Throughout the afternoon I sat in vigil alongside the cot as various members of both families bobbed their heads round the door. I didn't want to speak to anyone; in fact felt too numb to speak.

Finally, the young doctor who had tried to take the blood sample in the morning appeared. He apologised but gently explained that he had to establish that Gregory was dead.

'I should have thought that was obvious,' Ross replied bitterly, and this time I felt a surge of pity for this young doctor as a look of sadness registered on his face as he checked Gregory's vital signs.

There was no breathing, no pulse, no heartbeat, no sign of life.

After the doctor had left, I stared once more at the body of my son. His face which had contorted upon death was peaceful now, the muscles of his face relaxed, eyes closed, mouth gaping open. I held his tiny hand in mine for hours as it grew colder and colder, the previously pink nail bed of his tiny fingernails beginning to turn blue.

With a start, I noticed that it had grown dark outside the window and I realised that I felt so stiff that I would have to move. I reluctantly released my grip on Gregory's body, which had now grown hard and cold.

Ross asked gently then whether I was ready to go home.

I was so stiff from sitting motionless for so many hours that I was unable to move easily so Ross helped me to dress.

For the first time in days I dressed in day clothes, rather than the night clothes I had previously been wearing – preparing myself once more to enter the outside world.

Taking a final look back at Gregory from the doorway of the room we seemed to have spent so much time in, I knew that I was leaving the hospital to re-enter a world forever changed for me.

A Moment of Peace

As we left the hospital where Gregory had spent his short life, the walls of the corridors seemed to mock; silent screams of suffering child patients convincing me that I was an atheist, despite having been indoctrinated into the Roman Catholic religion as a child.

There was *no God,* there could be no higher being who would let children suffer the torments that we had seen so many suffer. I had only been at the hospital for a matter of days, but had experienced such a harrowing time, that I felt as though I had been imprisoned within its walls for an eternity. I felt that I had experienced so much that I could be emerging from a long prison sentence to a world completely changed.

I was no longer the person I had been only a few days before.

In the short time since I had left home to go into Macclesfield hospital to give birth, I felt that I had experienced a whole lifetime's worth of hardship and sorrow.

I knew that I was leaving behind in Manchester the body of a child who had he have lived would undoubtedly have caused us a lifetime of difficulty and pain, but I also felt that I should be returning home with a baby who should have become a child, adolescent, then man; who we had expected to bring us a lifetime of joy.

The staff gave Ross a sleeping pill for me to take when I got home, telling him that I should go straight to bed, and that they would contact my GP to make a home visit for the following morning. His twin brother, Lee, who had travelled from Scotland to be with him, drove us home, through the squalid streets of the city and into the suburbs, then to our home in Knutsford.

No words were exchanged on the journey.

Once home, Ross went around the house, turning on lights and heating. It was cold and bleak, and no longer felt like home. I struggled to climb the stairs to get to the bedroom, desperate to be alone with my thoughts. Perversely, although I felt physical pain from the caesarean section, I was so numb with shock that this didn't register, but only slowed my progress up the stairs.

As Ross and Lee sat downstairs, drinking whisky and talking in hushed tones, I swallowed the sleeping pill, wishing that I had a whole bottle, feeling that if I had, I would have happily swallowed the lot.

I drifted into a light sleep - the first time for days, as I had been unable to sleep in hospital, where so many worries had flooded my mind and tortured me.

I don't know how long I was in this state of light slumber, but suddenly I felt clear-headed and wide awake. I felt as though I bolted upright against the pillows, into a sitting position, as a bright light at the foot of the bed flooded the room.

For the first time since leaving home to go into hospital to have my baby I felt a feeling of peace descend over me. It enveloped the whole of my body with warmth, from the top of my head to the tips of my toes.

In that instant I *knew* that Gregory was in the room with me.

As I looked into the silver-blue light it changed shape, and seemed to take on wings.

I felt very calm, and very *sure* that although I had left the physical body of my baby behind in hospital, that he was now in the room with me.

A feeling of immense happiness overcame me.

I now knew that he was safe and that he wanted me to let him go.

He had come to say goodbye.

With what I can only clumsily describe as a beating of wings, the light spiralling upwards, my baby departed this life, *I feel*, finally at peace.

I had never previously experienced anything like this before and never since; despite on many subsequent occasions consciously trying to mentally conjure up some feeling of contact with my dead son.

I am unable to offer any rational explanation for what happened that night, but only know that the experience was real; as real as any other experience. I had left hospital convinced that I was an atheist after seeing what my baby had endured, and knew that this could not be a conscious religious experience that I would wish for. Perhaps a psychiatrist might explain it as being a consequence of stress, a hallucination of some kind, perhaps brought about by altered chemicals in the brain, causing a different state of mind; perhaps it was simply a vivid dream, or an effect of the sleeping pill I had taken.

But, I *know* that the experience was real.

I have never been as sure of this as anything in my life. I don't know whether I was awake or asleep, but I know that what I experienced was as real and tangible as anything else I have ever experienced.

A Time of Intense Pain

The following days leading up to Gregory's funeral were not only ones of profound grief, but also immense physical discomfort. My mind too numb to be able to articulate the loss, my body wept for me. As my breasts filled with milk, it spilt from my body as though weeping inconsolably for my loss. As I bled profusely, I didn't feel as though my body was repairing itself, but as though I was bleeding in pain for what I had lost.

As Ross busied himself with making funeral arrangements, I wandered the house, not knowing what to do with myself; although it was all I could do to cope with the physical aspects following the birth. I swallowed pills to dry up my breast milk, disposed of heavily soiled bloody pads, stained with lochia, and took diuretics for problems which had emerged towards the end of my pregnancy and for which I felt I had received insufficient medical help.

The midwife who came to take out my stitches was so unnerved in my presence that she left one behind, so I removed it myself. I developed an infection over the wound, which started to weep pus, and was given antibiotics to treat this.

I felt as though I would rattle with all the pills I had been given, but still couldn't wait for evening to arrive so that I could have a sleeping pill, which I found gave me a couple of hours - albeit tormented - rest.

I felt alone in bed; Ross now spending most of his time downstairs drinking either with his brother, who was staying at his parents' house, but visited as often as he was needed - or alone, as he didn't want to come to bed, as when he did manage to get to sleep he was tormented by nightmares.

I tossed and turned fretfully, and *willed* my son to visit again.

He did not.

It is impossible to describe how much I missed him.

His body remained at the hospital, awaiting a decision as to whether a post mortem would have to be carried out. We expressed a strong wish that his physical body should now be left alone; remaining untampered with in death, as it hadn't been in life. But I felt such a desperate craving to see or to have some contact again with Gregory, that against the advice of everyone close to me, including Ross, who also opposed this, I decided to go back to the hospital to see him. As I was so adamant that I was going to do this even if it meant getting a taxi, as I couldn't drive because of the caesarean section, Ross reluctantly agreed to drive me there, but told me that he might not want to see Gregory's body when we got to the hospital.

I assured him that this was fine with me; understanding that it was my desire that was compelling me to return. On arrival, we were told to go to the ward where Gregory had been nursed, where we talked to staff whilst preparations were made for me to visit Gregory, who was in the mortuary.

I saw the ward anew.

I saw the tortured eyes of the mother who had kept a long bedside vigil at the side of her son who had been in a coma for the last nine months following a road accident, taking it in turns with her husband to sleep on a camp bed at his side each night should he show any signs of recovery. I saw the squat body of a badly deformed child in a wheelchair, with withered legs, misshapen head, but a ready smile – a child whose presence had so badly frightened me when I had arrived on the ward to join Gregory on my transfer from Macclesfield. This time I managed a very faint smile in return; and I now felt deeply ashamed that I had been horrified by her appearance when I first saw her.

I was gently guided by a nurse back to the room I had shared with Ross during our stay at the hospital - opposite the intensive care room where Gregory had been nursed: perhaps she thought that to see this room again might be cathartic in some way for me. I was shocked to see that it appeared so ordinary now and that not only did it have a window – my previous perception of it is of it as having been like a prison cell, but that there was a square of grass beyond this with a children's playground there. I had registered none of this properly over the previous days, despite the fact that I had been there day and night - constantly alert - and had left the room only to be with Gregory; leaving the ward itself only once during that time at Ross's instigation, to visit the canteen for a ten minute break.

The same nurse accompanied us to the

mortuary, which was in an outbuilding away from the main hospital. As she unlocked the door an icy blast of cool air hit us. Supported by Ross, I walked in. Curtains enclosed cubicles, behind which I knew were the bodies of other children. There were so many ghosts crowded into the small room - clamouring to reclaim a lost childhood - and I could hardly breathe. I felt a vice like grip tightening around my throat. Gregory had been arranged for me to see him, probably also being enclosed behind a curtain too previously: but now placed at the top of the small room in a cradle enveloped with white drapes, with a teddy bear for company.

As I moved forward to stroke his cheek, which was yellow, as he had developed jaundice before his death, I knew that he was no longer there, and that what I was touching could in fact be a china doll. And, this is what he now looked and felt like. Rigor mortis had set in, and his face beneath my fingers was hard and unbelievably cold.

I stepped back, shivering, realising that the whole room was icy cold, before turning on my heel and walking out. I had satisfied myself that he was no longer here, that all that was left was a physical shell, and I walked away; finally sure that all physical ties were broken.

I now felt even more physically ill, not only from where I had been cut in the operation, but a heavy dragging sensation seemed to be tearing at my insides, as though my body was ripping itself apart. It was all I could now do to stumble back to the car, as overwhelming emotions began to rise up and then flood my mind.

Previously the overall feelings I had mostly had, had been of numbness and shock.

We Say Our Goodbyes

Despite the fact that I had seen with my own eyes that Gregory was no longer here, that he was incontrovertibly dead, that night I again willed him to visit me. Again, he did not. Instead, the following day his body was brought from the hospital in Manchester to a funeral parlour in Knutsford. Despite the fact that I knew that he was now in the same town, within easy access, I felt no further desire to visit him, understanding in that short space of time that all that remained of him was his physical body.

Before we could have a funeral his birth and death had to be registered. Because he had been born in Macclesfield, Cheshire, but had died in Manchester, and we had to follow the necessary bureaucratic procedures as the paperwork became available, it transpired that we would have to register his death first, and wait a day or two more for the necessary paperwork to register his birth.

Several relatives stepped forward to do this for us, but Ross decided that he wanted to do it; reasoning that as we had had such a short time to do so little for our son, that this was the least we could do for him. Suddenly, I became overwhelmed with anger. I had carried and cared for this baby alone for nine months, but subsequently had had all responsibility and decisions for him and about him taken away from me, so I angrily resolved that I would do this one last thing, not only for him, but for *myself*. I felt overwhelmed by a sense of wanting to assert some control over my own life again, feeling that all control had so cruelly been snatched from me.

Outside the Registry Office in Manchester, Ross checked with me that I was up to doing this. I felt sick with apprehension at the thought of what I was about to do, but felt sure that I needed to do this. Inside the office we both fumed with silent anger at the bureaucracy that the procedures entailed. In slow, laborious writing, the Registrar filled in the necessary forms and death certificate.

In the 'Cause of death' section the nib of her fountain pen laboriously scratched:

a. Respiratory Failure
b. Hydrocephalus + Meninomyelocoele (Spina Bifida)
c. Fetal Distress
d. Emergency lower segment Caesarean section
Certified by Nums – Sabah Ali   M.B.'

With my hand trembling almost uncontrollably I signed the certificate, indicating that to the best of my knowledge and belief that the particulars given were true.

Ross registered Gregory's birth the next day, when ironically the necessary paperwork, which would enable us to do this, arrived. He was able to do this locally, but I was by this time so bitter and traumatised by what had happened that I didn't have the heart to go with him to do this. After all, I thought, Gregory was dead, and I could summon up no enthusiasm, nor would I feel any joy in registering his birth. Ross also made most of the arrangements for the funeral. We were both in agreement that we wanted to have our son cremated, as the thought of him being buried, to decompose slowly over time was a thought neither of us could bear. As the earliest slot available at any local crematorium was at Macclesfield on Friday morning, we undertook the necessary procedures to book this, wanting now to get the funeral over and done with. This left us with very little time to organise it.

The most difficult obstacle to overcome was that neither of us wanted a religious service, but after all that had happened in the last week neither of us had the mental strength or the physical energy to devise our own service. After consultation with the undertaker, he approached a minister from a local church, who although he knew about our reservations that a religious service would be hypocrisy to us, laid aside any reservations he may have had, agreeing to conduct a simple service, with my father choosing a couple of hymns to accompany this.

In the days leading up to the service, I spent a lot of time in the nursery we had prepared for Gregory. Despite all my instincts wanting to destroy the room and tear the clothes we had prepared for him, I could not do so, aware of all the time and love which had gone into the preparation of this. In the early hours of the morning as I sat in there hugging my knees unable to sleep, I hit upon the idea that I would bring Gregory home.

As I voiced this the following morning, I could tell from Ross's face that he didn't want me to do this. As the day for the funeral approached, other relatives attempted to dissuade me from doing this too, without success. Finally, Ross agreed that if this was what I wanted to do that he would not stand in my way.

At dawn on the day of the funeral I stood at my bedroom window and watched a weak December sun slowly rise. As morning slowly broke on this new month, our closest relatives began to arrive at intervals at the house. I had nothing to say to any of them, remaining in my room alone, as our mothers busied themselves preparing for funeral guests who would be returning to the house for the wake. Eventually I washed and dressed, unmoved by this invasion of my home, to then return to my vigil at the window where I waited; hugging myself for want of a baby to hold.

I waited what seemed like hours before a limousine manoeuvred itself around the narrow corner of the street. As it stopped outside the house I strained to see where my son was, the car seeming empty but for the undertakers. I watched impassively as the undertaker carried the tiniest coffin I had ever seen down the path, still hugging myself. This was placed in the nursery, and someone bobbed their head round the door of my bedroom to ask whether I wanted the lid on the coffin sealed, or left off.

I asked for it to be left off, and with a heavy heart went to greet my son.

But it wasn't my son. What I saw was a

china doll, mouth gaping open, eyes tightly shut, and body rigid, cold and yellow. I touched his rock hard body and wondered what had happened to that moving, living child I had carried in my belly, whose first movement I had experienced as a flitting as gentle as a butterfly in my stomach, the baby whose elbow or leg had surfaced beneath my skin sharply prodding Ross when we lay together in bed, who could cause ripples on the surface of my teacup if balanced on my belly, the baby who had caused the strangest of sensations as he somersaulted, who caused such terrible indigestion, before pressing down so heavily that I could barely move with his weight. I had been so convinced that he was healthy. He had seemed so full of life.

There he was, dead, in a tiny coffin before me. I could scarcely believe that he could have been so alive when I was carrying him, but dead now. I sat with him, stroking him until the undertaker arrived to seal the coffin.

Ross asked that his brother travel with us to the crematorium and the three of us sat together with the coffin jarring against our knees. I stared out of the window of the car, and those travelling in other cars stared back. I felt numb.

Suddenly, as a strong ray of sunshine lit the sky, I felt indescribable anger that the sun should shine when my son was dead.

As we arrived at the cemetery, groups of relatives and friends stood in silence, heads bowed, as we sat locked in the car whilst the undertakers then ushered everyone inside. They then unlocked the doors of the hearse and asked how we wanted the coffin taken into the crematorium. With one swoop, Ross lifted the coffin into his arms, and weeping inconsolably turned to me and said with a bitterness I had never seen in him before, 'I had expected our children to bury us, not us to bury them.'

These words and his expression are seared in my memory.

Entering the crematorium, family and friends wept openly and noisily as I followed Ross carrying the coffin containing the body of our son. I think that I was the only person in the room who didn't cry. I followed as though completely detached from everyone and everything.

Although dry-eyed, I felt overwhelmed by pain; the likes of which I had never experienced before and which words alone cannot explain.

It was indescribable, a pain which was *too deep for tears.*

Loneliness

To the strains of the words of the traditional popular Christian hymn, 'All Things Bright And Beautiful,' chosen by my dad for the funeral, I stared uncomprehendingly at Gregory's tiny coffin at the front of the crematorium. Dad sang loudly and clearly, the strength in his voice seeming to show a determination to celebrate Gregory's short life:

'All things bright and beautiful,
All creatures great and small,
....'

All thoughts were obliterated as his voice rose loudly above the rest of the congregation, revealing nothing of the sorrow which he must have been feeling, but instead singing with such gusto and praise that no-one could doubt that he was celebrating his grandson's short life, and in the process perhaps possibly trying to imbue in us the courage to cope with the service – and our loss. I focused on the words as he sang:

'...
The purple-headed mountain,
The river running by,
The sunset and the morning,
That brightens up the sky;
....'

At these words, I finally broke down in choking

sobs as memories flooded my mind from the previous week when Gregory had been born at Macclesfield hospital, just around the corner from the cemetery. He had been born on the morning of the 22nd November as a weak winter sun had slowly begun to cast its light over a new day, and with this new day had come a new life.

And yet now, such a short time later – on 1st December, we were holding a funeral for a life which had been snuffed out seemingly with the ease with which one can blow out a candle; but who had been through so much in such a relatively small amount of time that I felt as though he, and us too, had experienced a *lifetime* of sorrow in the intervening days.

If I hadn't taken him home and seen him in the coffin with my own eyes, I would scarcely have been able to believe that all that remained of my living, kicking baby was his physical body lying in the coffin in front of us.

The words of the minister who was conducting the service escaped me as I became lost in my own thoughts about my son. From time to time, I noticed the minister's lips moving as he spoke words I did not hear. I also noticed that his eyes always seemed to be on my face. I made no attempt to make eye contact with him, lost in feelings of sadness which threatened to engulf me.

Another hymn began, the undertaker himself playing the music to accompany this on an organ. This one I had chosen with dad earlier in the week, initially not being particularly interested in which hymns were sung, but at the last minute choosing this, as it was so familiar from all the times I had heard it as a child when attending Sunday mass. It had also been one of the hymns sung at our wedding, so it seemed an appropriate connection to Gregory. It was the Jan Struther hymn 'Lord of All Hopefulness,' and as once again dad sang loudly and clearly I focused on his words.

'Lord of all hopefulness, Lord of all joy,
Whose trust, ever child-like, no cares could destroy.
Be there at our waking, and give us, we pray,
Your bliss in our hearts, Lord, at the break of the day.

Lord of all eagerness, Lord of all faith,
Whose strong hands were skilled at the plane and the lathe.
Be there at our labours, and give us, we pray,
Your strength in our hearts, Lord, at the noon of the day.

Lord of all kindliness, Lord of all grace,
Your hands swift to welcome, your arms to embrace.
Be there at our homing, and give us, we pray,
Your love in our hearts, Lord, at the eve of the day.

Lord of all gentleness. Lord of all calm,
Whose voice is contentment, whose presence is balm.
Be there at our sleeping, and give us, we pray,
Your peace in our hearts, Lord, at the end of the

day.'

Every word of this hymn seemed pertinent to me, and if I had abandoned the religion I had been brought up with, I certainly felt like it had now also abandoned me. Never had I felt as alone as I did on that day. It was as though there was a gaping emptiness inside me; and I suppose that in actuality there was – the emptiness where Gregory had been.

As the curtains closed on his coffin, it was all I could do to stop myself from crying out and flinging myself at the tiny coffin. Instead, I was gently guided outside by many pairs of hands. In turn family, friends and work colleagues offered us their condolences. Most found it difficult to speak and I couldn't find any words to say to them.

And then, I became overwhelmed by emotion, feeling deeply touched as two of the nurses who had nursed Gregory at Booth Hall Children's Hospital stepped forward and hugged me. At last I felt a human connection. Although I had known my family and friends throughout life, no-one other than me and Ross had known Gregory as well as these nurses; and I was touched and grateful that they had attended his funeral.

It struck me then as ironic that no-one from Macclesfield hospital had attended, despite the proximity of the hospital to the cemetery. I quickly pushed this thought from my mind as the undertaker asked what we wanted to do with the flowers which had been sent. We had asked that donations be sent to Booth Hall Children's Hospital instead of flowers, but we had also received a couple of sprays of flowers, one brought by the nurses from Booth Hall hospital.

I asked that some should go to Macclesfield hospital, preferably to someone who was having a difficult time there, and that others should go to St Cross Church in Knutsford as the minister from there had been so kind, conducting the service as though we were his congregation, despite not knowing us, and despite the fact that he knew that Ross and I did not follow any religion.

Back at home, our mothers busied themselves making tea and sandwiches for those who had returned with us to the house for the wake. I slumped in a chair, feeling physically exhausted and mentally drained. The noise from the guests' voices hummed indecipherably in my ears. Declining anything to eat or drink, I watched as Ross drank whisky with his friends. Occasionally, a chortle of restrained laughter escaped the group. Although I noticed this, I did not care. Life was going on as normal.

It was *my* life which felt so changed.

As conversations in various groups ebbed and flowed I sat alone, surrounded by family, relatives and friends and, thus surrounded by everyone I knew, I felt lonelier than I had ever believed it possible to feel. As one of six children, even from being a small child I had always valued my own space, never minding being alone, but today I learned the difference between being alone and being *lonely*. It is possible to feel immense loneliness even when in a crowd of people.

I slipped out of the room, wanting to be alone now, and made the laborious climb up the stairs to my bedroom, intending to lie down. As I entered the room I noticed with frustration that I couldn't even do that as our bed was piled high with the coats of visitors.

I sank to my knees, gasping in sobs. Suddenly, I noticed that there were two other people on their knees on the floor, one either side of me. It was my two oldest friends, Linda and Jane. No words passed between us, but they both hugged me. Eventually, having grown stiff from kneeling we returned downstairs just as everyone was beginning to leave.

As quickly as the house had filled it emptied, only a few close relatives remaining now.

Once everywhere had been tidied the remaining relatives now also began to depart. Among those last to leave were Ross's mum and dad, who were taking his great aunt Jenny home. At the door as we were saying goodbye, I heard great aunt Jenny ask his mum, 'Is she going to be alright Sylvia? I am so worried about her.'

I looked into her eyes then and saw a reflection of *my pain*. I knew in that instant that she had also suffered some loss.

Although we had known that her sister Bella had had a baby with spina bifida, and had given this information to the midwife when I booked in to the ante natal clinic, we had believed that Jenny had had no children. Even Ross's mum, who was very close to all her family and believed she knew all the family history, was surprised when a couple of weeks later the news emerged that Jenny had given birth to a stillborn baby, her only child. This baby had been immediately taken from her at birth and wrapped in a blanket before she had chance to see or hold him or her; the doctor believing this the right thing to do as he realised that the baby had spina bifida. From that day on Jenny had kept this *secret shame* to herself, only a few close members of her family knowing this, the knowledge almost disappearing from family history as time had passed.

We had always thought that she couldn't have children, but looking at her standing on the doorstep on the day of Gregory's funeral everything about how she lived her life and conducted herself; including the rather distant relationship which seemed to exist between her and her husband, seemed to slot into place.

Unfortunately, she was never able to talk to me about her child. I cannot speak for her, but can only hazard a guess that having carried this burden of sadness into old age, that she did not want to discuss it at the end of her life. She carried this sadness to her grave; only sharing the bald fact that she had had a baby with spina bifida to Ross's mum when we needed this information for genetic counselling.

No-one knows whether she had a son or daughter, or, indeed, whether she even knew herself, nor whether her baby had been named or had received a proper burial, or whether the body had been simply disposed of.

The actions of our predecessors, although previously probably *considered* correct; the medical profession probably sincerely believing that this was the best way to act to spare the feelings of a mother who had ended up in such a situation, today, seem to me to be unbelievably cruel.

I closed the door behind great aunt Jenny on the day of Gregory's funeral without fully understanding the reason for the *pain* etched upon the face of this slight woman, who looked as frail as a tiny bird – but I certainly *shared* it.

A Shared but Separate Grief

If the days passed slowly, the nights seemed to be never ending. It seemed as though we were just going through the motions of living. Our emotions would change on a minutely basis. They swung wildly, from numbness to sadness, from grief to anger, leaving us both permanently exhausted.

Now that the funeral was over, we had little to do, Ross's employers persuading him to return slowly to work, to go in as and when he felt up to it, gradually building to going back full time.

As everything had happened so fast, this time became a source of confusion, not only for us but for others too. We received telephone calls and cards congratulating us on the birth of our son from people who didn't know that he had died. We were grief stricken to read these messages of congratulations, but I kept the cards knowing that they had been sent with kindness. After all, no-one expects a baby to die. Birth is usually a time for celebration and what had happened to us didn't seem to make any sense.

The natural order of the world had been turned upon its head.

Day after day passed in this grief stricken way and everything about life seemed to be completely futile. We tried to get back to our previous routine as quickly as possible, but this wasn't easy. Although I bathed, I did not put on make up or take care in doing my hair as I would have previously. I ate, but not often, all food tasting dry, and threatening to choke me as I could not contain the sobs which seemed to come often and unexpected.

In Booth Hall Children's Hospital I had wondered whether our relationship would survive what had happened to us. Obviously no parent would wish for a disabled child, but from Gregory's birth it was as though I had had to plea bargain in my own mind about what might be acceptable.

As time had passed with Gregory on life support, I had decided in my own mind that physical handicap would be lamentable but acceptable, but over the long hours of those early days I had reasoned that I didn't want to have a child who would only know pain and would have no quality of life.

From Gregory's birth I didn't feel that I could live without him, but I was also sure that I could not endure watching a child experience a life full of pain and without quality, a child who would be looked upon with pity by society. I had thought about splitting up my marriage, and living alone somewhere with Gregory if he could have some quality of life, figuring that there was no point in both Ross's *and* my life being determined by the needs of a disabled child.

I had also planned that if Gregory's problems were so severe that he would live in a vegetative state that I would smother him with a pillow, and felt at that time that I could *do* this if it would spare Gregory a lifetime of pain. I hadn't told anyone about these thoughts, fearing that if I did that Gregory would be made a ward of court, and responsibility for his life taken away from me.

Now, after his death, I would spend whole nights mulling over these thoughts, unable to sleep. I desperately missed Gregory, in a way I imagined a person might feel at the loss of a limb, and as I thought of him, I felt sharp pains shooting through my body, perhaps nerve endings repairing themselves from where I had been operated upon.

As I felt sharp pins and needles shooting through my body, from my head to the tips of my toes, I felt as though I was not going to properly recover from this experience.

It was as though some fundamental part of me had stopped functioning properly.

However, I was glad to experience this physical pain as it occasionally took my mind off the grief I was feeling.

Words flooded my mind. At that time some words which I think were from a Bob Dylan song, probably distorted, echoed over and over in my mind as I lay awake in bed:

'I can cook and sew
Make flowers grow
Do you understand my pain?'

DO YOU UNDERSTAND MY PAIN?

I doubted that anyone possibly could.

I knew that Ross was also suffering as he would often wake up drenched in sweat from a nightmare. He told me that his nightmares usually featured images of very deformed children. In one, he vividly recalled a horrific scene of the bodies of dead children who were disabled or ravaged by some dreadful disease all piled one on top of another, as though assembled as a bonfire, waiting to be burnt.

He had so many nightmares at this time that he began to dread going to bed, and would often sit up drinking whisky. I had been given some sleeping pills, so usually got some sleep, but it was a sleep which didn't feel natural; and I would often wake in the early hours feeling very tired but, unable to get back to sleep, wishing that Gregory would come to me as he had on the night he had died. He did not.

We received a letter from the social worker at Macclesfield hospital asking us whether we needed any counselling. We declined this, although I decided to return to the hospital to retrace my steps to see whether my memories of the place were accurate.

I was impassive as I did this, and saw once again the room I had been in during labour, the theatre and SCBU and the ward I had been put on after Gregory's birth. I decided that short of waving a magic wand and going back in time to change events that she could not help me.

A lady who did help a little was a lady from ASBAH, the Association for Spina Bifida and Hydrocephalus, named Elizabeth Lawlor. She visited on a couple of occasions and clarified questions which were now beginning to surface about the disability.

On one occasion when I knew she was to

visit that morning, I was feeling so low that I stayed in bed, not wishing to see her, or anyone else for that matter. I was particularly nasty to Ross, lashing out at him in anger when he urged me to get up to see her. As I heard her tread on the stairs and her approach to the bedroom I pulled the duvet over my head and decided to ignore her.

As she gently coaxed me to speak to her, I emerged from the duvet just for long enough to tell her to 'piss off.' She quietly uttered the words, 'poor lamb,' before disappearing downstairs to talk to Ross.

As I heard them speaking in hushed tones I felt immense anger, and hated everyone and everything in the world, including myself.

I could not make any connection with Ross at this time. All I longed for was to have my baby back. The longing was not only emotional, but was so physical that it hurt. I hated Ross with a vengeance, knowing that he wasn't experiencing this physical longing in the same way as I was, as my hormones played havoc with both my mind and body. Despite the fact that he had been a good husband and father, I felt that I was experiencing a grief that he could not possibly understand. I resented the fact that his life was resuming some semblance of normality, while mine seemed to be spiralling more and more out of control. I resented the fact that he was able to go out to work and carry on everyday activities in a more normal fashion than I felt I was able.

Despite this, somewhere deep inside I knew that I still loved my husband and that what I

177

was experiencing was grief. I also *knew* that he was grieving deeply too – and on some level I think that I understood that he envied me the space I had to grieve, knowing that he had to resume work and *feeling it a burden to do so*, so soon after the loss of his only child.

Incomprehension and Fear

Each time I fell asleep, I would jerk awake with my heart pounding and a terrible cloud of dread hanging over me. I felt as though caught in a thick fog, unsure of where I was and what was happening, although I knew that I was in a place I didn't want to be. After a minute or two, I would feel a dreadful feeling of loss overtake me as gradually each time on awakening I would recall recent events anew.

Different emotions assaulted me, with the force of strong waves; threatening to engulf me in their current, dragging me down into the deepest depths of despair, hopelessness or anger. I also experienced another, *overwhelming* feeling, of fear.

This fear was all encompassing. It didn't matter where I was, or whether I was with someone, or alone – this fear permanently lurked. It was such a physical feeling that I felt as though I would have a heart attack or a stroke, as my heart pounded wildly and my head throbbed with such force that it was as though I could physically feel the blood pulsing in my ears and behind my eyes, deafening me to all rational thought and blinding me to all ordinary activities.

Rational thought had completely escaped me. Although I felt somewhere in the deep recess of my mind that the worst had already happened, I couldn't reconcile myself to anything. Emotions of all kinds rolled over me, in the same way as waves roll in the sea, unstoppable, rising to a crescendo, sometimes simply lapping in the background, but always there, unbidden, as uncontrollable and cyclical as nature itself.

Academics have identified different stages of grief. Elizabeth Kubler-Ross identified the commonly accepted five stages of Denial, Anger, Bargaining, Depression and Acceptance as being the emotional experiences which characterise grief.

All that I know is that I experienced all these emotions – and more. I didn't experience them in any set order, nor for a specified amount of time. My grief was erratic, different emotions overwhelming me at any time and for different amounts of time. It was messy, my body recovering from childbirth and yet craving intimacy with the person I was most close to, my husband – with whom I quickly and surprisingly naturally restored a sexual relationship, which defied logic considering what we had been through, although I feel that I was craving the physical closeness I should have been experiencing with my baby.

My grief was emotional. It was physical. It ebbed and it waned, but it was always permanently there, manifesting itself in one form or another. There was no escaping it. No activity could distract me from it. It was with me day and night, awake or asleep; it was there on a conscious level, or working itself subconsciously to the surface of my thoughts even when asleep.

Unlike Ross, I didn't have nightmares about

Gregory, but was simply aware of the effects of his monumental loss. Although rationally I had previously reconciled myself to the thought that it would be for the best if he died, now that he had died his loss was overwhelming. I had not been able to imagine living with him, but now I couldn't cope with the reality of living without him.

Nothing seemed to matter any more. Everything about life was perfunctory, including all my relationships. Even though I had lived with Ross for so many years without children, now that we had had a child, our relationship had changed. Without Gregory it was as though we were simply going through the motions of living.

Nothing in life had prepared me for the intensity and depth of the feelings I was now experiencing. I remember this as a terrible time. I wanted to escape these feelings, or at least to find some respite from them, but there was none to be had.

If I went into town I would invariably meet one of the other mum's from the ante natal group I had attended. The first I encountered was struggling with a pram on the narrow pavement and greeted me in a distracted but cheery way with the words, 'Lucky you – to be out on your own so soon. Who is looking after your baby? What did you have?'

I could scarcely find the words to reply to her question and felt stigmatised by my lack of a baby. I expect that news of what had happened to me quickly spread through our small community, so I gave up going into town as it distressed me so much, and I began to go into larger surrounding towns if we needed any shopping, hoping that I wouldn't bump into anyone I knew and have to explain what had happened. This didn't help much. I recall on one occasion being in a Boots shop somewhere and despite the fact that *I* was anonymous, I felt such a fierce surge of anger overtake me that I wanted to sweep all the baby products from the shelves there.

In a supermarket, Sainsbury's in Wilmslow, walking past the meat counter I noticed oxtail for sale there. The sight of this reminded me of seeing Gregory's exposed spine after his birth; and I was so upset by this that my basket crashed to the ground as I ran out of the shop unable to control my emotions.

It was now approaching Christmas and towns and shops bustled with activity. The ornate window displays, and trees bedecked with lights and other decorations, seemed to mock me in their gaudiness, and I felt dizzy and sick as strings of coloured lights strewn across the streets of every town blew in the wind, puddles reflecting in ripples their bright colours.

The noise of Noddy Holder's gruff voice from Slade's Christmas song, 'Merry Xmas Everybody' screamed out:

'It's CHRRIIIIISSS-MASSS!'
seemingly every shop doorway I passed.
The song thundered on loudly:

'So here it is merry Christmas
Everybody's having fun

Look to the future now
It's only just begun ...'

For me there was no fun and my head span
with these words as I couldn't see a future for
me.

The rock band Wizzard's song, 'I Wish It
Could Be Christmas Everyday,' also seemed to
be repeatedly playing: the words, 'Let the bells
ring out for Christmas,' haunting me wherever I
went. I felt that the only bell which should ring
was to toll the death of my son.

But, of course, strangers passing in the street
couldn't possibly know how I was feeling. I
wanted to *scream* out that I had lost my son. I
wanted to wear my grief like a coat so that they
would understand how I was feeling; and I
lamented the fact that in some societies grief is
more ritualistic than it is in ours, with the
bereaved observing certain customs, such as
wearing black for a period, or behaving in
certain ways to mourn their lost one, so that
others should know that they were in mourning
and respect this.

There was no escape from what appeared to
me then as this *enforced* jollity. I stopped
turning on the TV, and eventually the radio too,
as tears would drip unbeckoned when I heard
more tender words, such as those of singers such
as Cliff Richard singing songs such as 'Mistletoe
and Wine':

'A time for living, a time for believing
A time for trusting, not deceiving,
Love and laughter and joy ever after,

Ours for the taking, just follow the master.'

As nativity plays were re-enacted up and down the land celebrating the Christian birth of baby Jesus, nothing could console me for the loss of *my* son. His loss seemed to be accentuated by the time of year that it had happened – a time of year when Christians celebrate new life; and others simply celebrate what is for us probably our most popular celebration of the year.

I did take comfort from the cards we received, particularly those which contained a message acknowledging our loss. A few people were brave enough to telephone us to express their condolences, and although I would always end up in tears, I appreciated the courage which it must have taken to do this.

We drew most comfort from the messages which seemed to understand the enormity of the loss which we were feeling. These invariably came from others who had lost loved ones. Ross found one such message waiting for him on his desk in his office when he returned to work. Touching in its simplicity, it expressed everything that we were feeling. It read:

'Dear Ross

I was so sad to hear about your loss.
I lost a daughter when she was 3 so I know that nothing can hurt as much as the death of one of your children.

Kind regards
Chris'

A managing editor, Ruth, from a publishing house that I worked for, kindly sat down and wrote to me a lengthy letter about the death of her husband, and I reproduce here some of the words which gave me a little hope for the future and made me feel less isolated in my grief:

'... the cliché that time heals really is true. The cliché makes more sense if I express it the way my doctor did when I went to see him about three months after Tom died. I was getting tired of bursting into tears almost every day when I felt I should be beginning to get better, and wailed, "When is the pain going to go away?" and he replied, "It won't go away but it will change – it will just become part of you and it will feel OK ...".'

The words which most deeply touched me came from a spinster with no children of her own, a colleague of Ross's, called Mon, and I was surprised that a lady with no children could so accurately sum up what we were feeling and offer such comfort:

' ... I can't begin to imagine what you must both be feeling and hope that the hurt will ease a little each day.
I was glad that you had been able to hold and cuddle Gregory at the end so that you could feel he was truly yours for his short life. I am sure that in that short life he became your first son and was loved.'

As I read this, all anger about the loss of our son

evaporated for me at that time; as I began to understand - for the first time, that Gregory would live on forever in my heart and mind. I came to believe the little known words of St John Chrysostorn, a bishop from the fourth century, who expressed it thus:

'He whom we love and lose is no longer where he was before. He is now wherever we are.'

Nonetheless, despite all of this, there was a gaping hole in my life and it was painful to go into the nursery only to find an empty cradle there. Even my friend Linda's small children could acknowledge, if not fully *understand*, the loss. Linda had three children, and, thankfully, brought them with her when visiting, understanding that it would be more painful for me if she did not.

On arrival at their first visit Emma, the eldest, asked me very sombrely whether I was *very sad* that my baby had died, before asking if she and her brother, Robert, could look at the nursery. Trooping down the stairs after doing this, they then sat in the living room heads bent over a piece of paper as one of them drew a cradle, and then drew inside this a picture of a baby's head poking over a blanket, suggesting in all their childhood innocence and naivety that I place a doll in the cot for comfort. Then, their attention being redirected towards themselves quickly, as it always is with small children, they drew images of themselves on the same paper, but added down-turned mouths to their faces to indicate their sadness. The last image they drew was of the latest addition to their family, a baby called Andrew.

Suddenly, the middle child, Robert, our godson, hit upon the ingenious idea of giving Andrew to us as a gift, which brought what I think must have been the first smile to my face since Gregory had died, as I realised the sibling rivalry he was probably feeling at being replaced as the baby in his family.

Emma responded angrily, 'Oh *W*obert, you are a silly boy. Now you will upset mummy as well. Don't you remember we were to be good and not say anything to upset Fran ... and now you will have upset mummy ... you are a *silly* boy.'

As I waved them goodbye, I could feel a smile tugging at the corners of my lips, and I realised with surprise that I felt more cheerful than at any time since Gregory had died!

Only a moment later my feelings changed. Before their car had even rounded the corner, I watched its tiny occupants, whose heads were scarcely visible despite the height provided by booster seats, but whose small hands waved vigorously, with a sadness and fear which threatened to overwhelm me — as I wondered whether *we* would ever experience the joy of having such a family. The prospect seemed to be so remote that upon closing the door, I slid to the floor and became engulfed in bitter and angry sobs.

Falling 'through the Net'

Dozing fitfully, I awoke to the noise of a bang which sounded like gunfire. For a moment I was confused by this, having no idea where I was, or what was happening. As I struggled for some recall, the whole place seemed to erupt with noise and light. Whistling and crackling explosive noises screeched through the air, tearing through the dark sky, so that it became ablaze with rainbow-coloured stars fizzing in downpours. The bedroom which had previously been in complete darkness became aglow with strange shadows of light and colour, reflecting eerily on the walls and ceiling despite the curtains and window being firmly closed against the night.

As quickly as these whistles and explosions had begun to rend the air, seeming to rattle at the very foundations of the house, a cascade of voices spontaneously erupted in wild whoops and cheers. It was New Year's Eve, and suddenly the whole town - earlier seeming to lie dormant in a stupour of winter bleakness - seemed to awake and pour out onto the streets to celebrate the arrival of not only a new year but also a new decade.

I pulled the pillow over my face and ears to block out the noise and light, feeling grief stricken. Although I was glad the year was over, I felt nothing but sadness as I recalled what had happened, and thought that the future too now looked very bleak. I also felt very sorry for us in our isolation, feeling that we were the only people in town who were not out celebrating. Instead, we had gone to bed early - at nine o'clock - when I had taken a sleeping pill, desperate to sleep through the festivities. Ross got up and silently and without switching on any lights went downstairs.

I lay awake, the noise and light seeping into my consciousness despite the fact that I did not want it to, as silent tears began to wet the pillow as I lay immobile not knowing what to do with myself. My head thumped and my heart pounded in time to the noise of the fireworks, and as each cascade of coloured stars burst in fountains of light in the sky I felt pins and needles all through my body, and visualised these as mimicking the colours and shapes created by the flecks of gunpowder.

If Christmas had been difficult, the New Year brought no respite. What it did bring was lots of questions. Our earlier feelings of shock at what had transpired had now changed to questions as to why events had brought us to this situation. There had been no indication that anything had been wrong throughout pregnancy and I had been monitored throughout, complying with all the medical advice I had received, as well as taking good care of my health and - as I thought - that of the baby, so it seemed incomprehensible to us that events had transpired as they had.

We both fully understood that Gregory had died, and that he had been born with spina bifida. What we didn't understand was why this hadn't been picked up, particularly in light of the information I had provided the midwife with at the booking clinic. We also could not accept that the poor standard of care both me and Gregory had received could be considered clinically acceptable under the health system in place in our country.

It was for this reason that we approached both my obstetrician and the paediatrician who had cared for Gregory in a quest to discover more information about what had happened and why the standard of care had been so poor. Although both doctors met with us - and offered us their *condolences* at Gregory's death, we came away from these meetings understanding little more about what had happened than we already knew.

I found it painful that the obstetrician seemed dispassionate in her explanation that we – and I shall always remember her words – had simply 'slipped through the net,' with regard to the medical tests not having detected Gregory's problems. She compounded my sadness by adding that anyway, even if the spina bifida had been spotted on the later scan that it would have been too late to have a termination. There had been no discussion at any point of this. She reiterated the information which she had told me on the day of Gregory's birth, that the scans and the AFP test had been re-checked, and that they had not indicated that there was any problem. We came away from our meeting with her feeling that she had no idea at all as to how we were feeling.

The paediatrician was more compassionate, but also more defensive. She asked whether we intended to sue the hospital. This was an idea which had never entered our heads. We asked her why Gregory's spina bifida had been missed, both when he had been delivered and during his time in Special Care, particularly as we had seen for ourselves that it was so clearly visible. She told us that she hadn't been in theatre, but had come in from home on receiving a call about Gregory, so didn't know what had happened there, but could only *presume* that he hadn't been breathing when he had been delivered and that staff had *probably* focused all their efforts on getting him to do so.

We asked why she hadn't *examined* him in an attempt to determine what his problem was, and she replied that the focus had been on getting him to breathe, and that during her time with him that he had been nursed on his back throughout, remaining in this position even when he had a chest X-ray to try to discover *why* he wouldn't breathe. Her final comment, added rather sheepishly, was that anyway he didn't *look* like a baby with spina bifida; indeed in appearance he did not seem to have any congenital abnormality.

Although the paediatrician was more compassionate in her attitude than the obstetrician, we were unhappy with the fact that she seemed to be urging us to simply accept the idea that, and these are her words – 'medicine is not an exact Science,' that we had been dealt a cruel blow by nature, and that there was nothing more to be said or done about what had happened.

We both came away from these meetings

feeling very unhappy with the whole situation. We wondered why I had gone through all the medical tests and spent so much time giving the midwife at the booking clinic a detailed family history, attended all the ante natal classes and medical examinations if not to ensure that the situation we had ended up in would not arise. We were both uncomfortable with the idea that Gregory's spina bifida had not been noticed in theatre, or had not been communicated to the paediatrician, and we wondered whether in reality there had been a breakdown in communication somewhere. We both also strongly felt that if Gregory had been examined that the cause of his problems would have been immediately apparent, and that events would not have taken the course that they had.

We found it very difficult to accept that given the number of staff in theatre when Gregory had been delivered that no-one there, and then subsequently in Special Care, had *noticed* Gregory's spina bifida, as when we had seen it only a few hours after his birth it was large in proportion to Gregory's size and it was bloodied, with bone and other spinal matter visible from a distance to the naked eye. We could not therefore accept that we should simply accept that nature had dealt us a cruel blow – which undoubtedly it had.

After much discussion we decided that we would complain to the hospital about the level of care which both Gregory and I had received, and that we would also ask them to answer questions which we felt had not been addressed, hoping that in this way we would find out more information than we had been given; and that perhaps if we outlined the poor standard of care that we had encountered that these problems could be rectified so that no-one else should have to suffer as we had.

Early in January we outlined all our concerns to Mr Jaycock, the Unit General Manager for Macclesfield, in a lengthy letter explaining everything that had happened. Knowing that it would take some time for these issues to be addressed, and now beginning to feel not only more grief-stricken but also exhausted by our efforts to obtain information, relatives urged us to take a break. Neither Ross nor I wanted to do this, feeling that it wasn't what we felt we wanted to do just then. We were though equally unsettled at home, questioning over and over what had happened. We didn't know what to do with ourselves.

Eventually, we were persuaded to take a break with a voucher which my friend Linda had been given for a short break in a hotel on The Isle of Wight. As neither of us had been there before and several relatives forced cash onto us to enable us to afford to do this, all our spare money having been spent on the nursery and the funeral, we reluctantly set off on this *holiday*.

It became important to us that everywhere we travelled then should be new to us, hoping that unhampered by memories we might be able to leave behind some of our grief. Of course we did not, carrying it with us as heavy as any baggage could ever be.

We spent a sad night in Devizes, Wiltshire,

simply because we had never been there before. The weather was as black as our mood, and as we travelled we listened to news bulletins on the radio which indicated that it was going to get worse. We set off the following morning for Salisbury, having eaten too little and drunk too much the previous evening. Neither of us had slept well, so were both feeling the worse for wear as we made our way across Salisbury Plain.

Passing through small villages and hamlets we didn't encounter a soul and turned on the car radio once more to obtain an update on the weather. On an hourly basis it seemed to be getting worse as the wind rose and rain began to lash the car. We passed areas of beech and coniferous woodland, the wind growing stronger all the time. As I watched the trees bending under its force, I felt that I would have been happy if one should be uprooted and crash across the car so that we could both be killed; putting an end to our misery.

We became aware of notices warning of the danger of straying into areas which are inaccessible to the public, the plain being one of the Ministry of Defence's and NATO's principal training grounds because of its sparse population. At that time I would have been happy if we had been blown up by an unexploded shell or mortar bomb, which litter the area.

As we travelled the road which cut across the plain I noticed a tank from the corner of my eye. It was travelling very quickly across the plain and it became obvious that it would cross the road we were travelling on at a point where we would be if we continued at the same speed we were doing now. I glanced at Ross to see if he had noticed the tank. He obviously had because his eyes strayed towards it now and then and then back ahead to the road. He did not alter his speed, but carried on driving, eyes firmly fixed now only on the road ahead.

I watched this tank, the huge treads covering its wheels looking very heavy, but moving swiftly across the terrain. It moved easily despite its huge size, entering and leaving craters in the ground, travelling across grassy areas or mud with ease. I wondered what it would feel like if it ran over the car, which judging by its size and momentum it could easily do. I thought that we would be crushed underfoot as easily as ants, and all that would remain would be a tangle of metal and crushed bodies.

As I was thinking this, I watched as the tank reached the road ahead of us and crossed it as we approached the point where it had done so. As quickly as it had appeared it disappeared into the distance beyond the other side of the road.

The weather was atrocious as we approached Salisbury where we decided to stop and have a break. Getting out of the car, I realised that I had left home without a coat or jacket of any kind. I think that this was indicative of my frame of mind at this time as I am usually an organised person. After bursting into tears of frustration and ineptitude we had to then spend the next hour looking for and purchasing a jacket suitable for the inclement weather. The sales assistant cut out all the labels from a wax jacket we eventually found, and once I had this on we decided that as we would probably never visit Salisbury again that we should take a look at its cathedral. We didn't spend very long doing this, as neither of us at this time could summon up any enthusiasm for the building, so we wearily returned to the car.

Ross studied his map searching for something which might capture our interest. I lay with my head on the headrest in the passenger seat, eyes closed, feeling immensely sad, uninterested in anything. All I could think of was my dead son.

Eventually, Ross decided that he would drive us to the New Forest, thinking that this might be of interest, as it dated back to William the Conqueror and was somewhere else we had never visited. Generally, we would have enjoyed a day out visiting this former royal hunting area with its habitat of unenclosed pasture land, heath land and forest, enjoying watching the deer and the semi-wild ponies and horses there. But nothing could arouse our interest today. We passed through small picturesque villages dotted around the area without giving them a second glance.

Throughout the journey we had been listening to the weather bulletins on the car radio and had heard that several ferries had been cancelled due to the adverse conditions. I wasn't at all worried by this news, not caring whether we got on a ferry or not, or indeed, if we did, whether it would sink.

I was in such a bad frame of mind at this

time that I cannot even remember whether we sailed from Southampton or Portsmouth, but do remember that when we arrived at the port all ferries had been cancelled as it was deemed too risky to sail. We spent the night in a small bed and breakfast in the town, which we left hurriedly early the following morning, not wishing to make small talk with the owners.

We took the first ferry to sail that day, and as it laboured its way through the dark choppy water, lurching alarmingly from side to side, rising and falling in the water like a fairground ride, I was pleased to feel and taste the tangy sea water stinging my face. The weather was no better on arrival at The Isle of Wight.

As we made our way across the island to our hotel everywhere was very quiet and the island seemed as inhospitable as our mood. The hotel we stayed in was basic and sparsely occupied. We avoided talking as much as possible to the owners and other guests – although there were so few of these that it was impossible not to become aware of each of them. Mostly they were older couples. There were no children there. I dreaded going to the dining room every night, where the owner languidly played soulless melodies on an old piano, which did nothing to bring any atmosphere to the cheerless room. If I hadn't felt so overwhelmed by dark feelings, I might otherwise have found the atmosphere humorous in some respect; but as it was, we ate little, and as quickly as possible, to escape to our equally cheerless room.

As I lay on my bed after dinner, the wind howling outside, rain lashing at the windows, the sound of the sea crashing thunderously on rocks below, I wondered what we were doing here. We just didn't seem to belong; but as I thought about this, I wondered if this would be the pattern of our holidays from now on – a miserable couple growing older and more miserable each year, taking holidays in remote hotels where there were no children to remind us of our dashed hopes. The idea depressed me beyond belief.

Despite the atrocious weather we went out walking at every opportunity. The spray from the sea mingled with the tears which rolled down my cheeks constantly. As I stood at the edge of the cliffs watching enormous, powerful waves crash onto the rocks below, with such force that it was scarcely credible that the rocks could withstand the battering, I wondered what it would feel like to throw myself from the cliff and put an end to the misery I was feeling. I pictured my body being dashed against the jagged rocks and figured that it couldn't feel any worse than I was feeling now.

Community News 'Exclusive'

I personally handed the letter of complaint to Mr Jaycock, asking at reception for directions to his office. Unknown to me there was a Health Authority meeting being held there that afternoon, and the receptionist, probably presuming I was attending this, simply waved me in the right direction without even looking up from her desk.

The first thing I noticed about the offices was the cleanliness of the carpets and the décor and that a cheery atmosphere pervaded, distinctly at odds with the sparse and clinical nature of the rest of the hospital.

I noticed Mrs Scott and Dr Shackleton; along with lots of others enter the office, before being approached by a secretary working in the outer office where I now was. I told her what my business was and she replied that Mr Jaycock was in an *important* Health Authority meeting and that she would give him my letter when this was finished. With a fire in my belly and anger in my heart which questioned just how important the patients and their facilities were at this hospital, I sat down on a chair and told her that she had better ask him to leave the meeting then for a moment. I decided in that short space of time that if he didn't, that I would join the meeting, taking my complaint to everyone there, as I was unlikely to get a better opportunity to have all these *important* people assembled together in one place.

My Jaycock left the meeting and after introducing myself and telling him why I was there I handed him the letter of complaint which he took, addressing me politely and assuring me that he would read it at the earliest opportunity. A few days later a formal letter of acknowledgment of the complaint arrived from his deputy, Diana Wakeman-Rose.

Unfortunately, so did a copy of a local newspaper – the *Community News*. It led on an 'Exclusive'. A large star outlined the words in capitals, 'COMMUNITY NEWS EXCLUSIVE.'

The headline in bold capitals read: **'MATERNITY SERVICES STARVED'**. The article was a byline by someone called Kath Hayward. I felt sick as I read the words reproduced here:

'Macclesfield maternity services are starved of essential funds by an uncaring administration says Obstetrics and Gynaecology Consultant, Mr David Mellor.

And patients are being sent home sometimes earlier than they would like because the West Park maternity unit has neither the space nor the midwives to care for them.

"We have had complaints from mums who feel they have been 'kicked out' too early," explained Mr Mellor. "And this is the last thing we want to happen. Here in Macclesfield we have a potentially very good service but we can't offer it to mums because of shortage of funds."

Constraints are placed on the service says

Mr Mellor by a shortage of trained midwives, shortage of beds (15 beds were closed earlier last year because of staff shortages) and the design of the maternity unit which is currently housed in buildings originally meant for another purpose altogether.

And, went on Mr Mellor, it isn't fair that a successful and expanding town like Macclesfield should have to "make do" when the rest of the town is booming.

If the town's population continues to grow then so will the demand for maternity services adds Mr Mellor. "When that happens we will be able to make a case for a new, purpose built unit. Until then we need to find ways of improving service – but we can't do this without expenditure."

When it comes to raising money for services Mr Mellor is a realist. "Of course the whole of the Health Service is short of cash – but there's no point spending money on administrators and computers if we can't afford to treat patients in the first place."

Referring to a recent cash deal with Stoke Health Authority which raised thousand of pounds for joint replacements at Macclesfield, Mr Mellor said: "We in the gynaecology team were very disappointed that at least some of the money – raised through performing hysterectomy operations on Stoke patients here at Macclesfield – did not come back into the unit and especially maternity. Surely some of the money would have been well spent on recruiting more midwives?"

At last month's meeting of Macclesfield

Health Authority Mr Jeff Jaycock presented a verbal report on the state of maternity services in the town.

"The closure of 15 beds in ward 20 in early summer has put too much pressure on the remaining beds on ward 19," he explained. "However, since that time the average length of stay has shortened from 5.5 days to 3.5 and using these figures, turnover interval and patient demand we are able to see the need to re-introduce six beds. Talks are now continuing with consultants to see if it is possible to fulfil this need by using a vacated delivery suite."

Recognising that the use of beds in the delivery suite is not the best answer, Mr Jaycock went on: "These beds would be used at the discretion of consultants while we look at long term plans. But we can only really improve facilities in the maternity unit by spending a lot of money – maybe now is the time to debate with the RHA on the possibilities of a new unit."

"It is not clinically acceptable to use beds, next door to the existing delivery suite, for the treatment of ante natal patients who need peace and quiet and somewhere to have their anxieties allayed," Mr Mellor went on.

"We are working hard to improve community care for ante-natal patients – for example we hope very shortly to introduce foetal monitoring at home so that patients don't have to be admitted unless it's really necessary – but it's no good having good community services if you haven't got the hospital unit back-up."

"Looking ahead what we want to do is create an environment in hospital which is as much like home as possible. Here in Macclesfield it is our philosophy to look at each patient as an individual in terms of treatment.

"We are completely against conveyor belt deliveries. But this building is simply not suitable to provide the privacy and isolation bays which are sometimes needed. The problem is that maternity services do not make money – demand for our services goes up and down – but we need to have the facilities here all the time in case of emergencies. And this does not make us popular with the administrators.'"

Ross was also to be upset by something he read. In the library at work one day he came across a 23 page report entitled: 'THE HEALTH OF THE POPULATION **MACCLESFIELD HEALTH AUTHORITY 1990,**' a copy of which he obtained for us to read at home. As we read, we realised with a sickening jolt that Gregory had become a *statistic* in this annual report of the Director of Public Health.

Under a section headed 'BIRTHS AND PROBLEMS IN INFANCY' it stated, 'There were 2,067 births to Macclesfield District residents in 1989, a small fall from a peak of 2,104 births in 1988. Just over half the children were born at Macclesfield District General Hospital ....'

Although not a statistician the following information presented under the heading, 'DEATHS TO BABIES AROUND THE TIME OF BIRTH AND IN THE FIRST YEAR OF LIFE,' hurt me to the core.

'Two mortality rates for babies are widely used internationally and attract much attention. The perinatal mortality rate is the number of stillbirths and deaths in the first week of life expressed as a proportion of all births. It is an indicator of the efficacy of antenatal care and care of newborn babies. The infant mortality rate, the proportion of live born babies who die in the first year, also reflects antenatal and neonatal care to some extent.

In Macclesfield in 1989 both the perinatal and infant mortality rates showed increases which initially gave rise to some comment. The District's perinatal mortality rate (8.2) was similar to the rates in Mersey Region and England and Wales, having been below regional and national rates since 1986. Fluctuations from year to year can be smoothed out by calculating five year average rates. These show that the downward trend in the perinatal mortality rate has slowed: 9.7 in 1982/86, 8.8 in 1983/87, 8.1 in 1984/1988, and 8.0 in 1985/89.
The infant mortality rate (11.2) is the highest since 1984 ...'

This was followed by two tables, one indicating perinatal mortality rates for 1982 to 1989, and the other indicating infant mortality rates for the same year. Below this were the comments reproduced here.

'Deaths around the time of birth are fortunately few and very small changes in numbers of deaths have a large impact on mortality rates.

An analysis of stillbirths and deaths in the first year of life showed that deaths in the first week of life accounted for most of the increases in both the perinatal and infant mortality rates in 1989.

Eleven first week deaths in 1989 represented an increase of three over the average for 1984 to 1988. Though all the babies died at hospitals outside the district, five of them were born in Macclesfield District General Hospital and were transferred for intensive care. Four of the eleven deaths were among babies with severe congenital malformations. ... With such small numbers it is difficult to draw conclusions.

However, across Europe the general fall in the perinatal mortality rate has been attributed to three main factors: antenatal diagnosis of certain congenital malformations with the offer of termination of pregnancy, including deliveries when pregnancies run into problems, and intensive care of premature infants. These factors imply that good antenatal and neonatal care are both important in preventing perinatal deaths.'

Bureaucracy

Feeling disappointed by the attitude of staff and administrators, who seemed to be at loggerheads over every aspect of the maternity services on offer at the hospital, Ross and I decided that we should bring this situation to the knowledge of our local MP, and the MP for the Macclesfield district where the hospital was situated. Consequently, we sent letters to Mr Neil Hamilton, who at that time was MP for the Tatton district where we lived, and Mr Nicholas Winterton for the Macclesfield district.

We received a speedy response from both; Mr Hamilton promising in the first instance to write on our behalf to the Chairman of the Macclesfield Health Authority, and also assuring us that he would do everything he could to ensure that there was a full and extensive enquiry into what had taken place. Mr Winterton extended his sympathies to us on our bereavement, but his letter continued:

'There is a strict Parliamentary tradition that Members do not become involved in correspondence with the residents of other constituencies and I very much regret, therefore, that you must pursue this case through your own Member of Parliament, Neil Hamilton, who will, I am confident, do all that he can to assist you.'

We were already beginning to think that we

would be pushed from pillar to post by all the different professionals we had approached to help us, and in a very short space of time had obtained a glimpse into the fact that they seemed to have no interest in working *together* for the service of the patients, but seemed more preoccupied with their own individual roles.

We realised with a feeling of dismay that we were going to have a battle on our hands. We were not seeking retribution, but strongly felt that we needed to *understand* what had happened to Gregory. We had had such a short time with him that it became of the utmost importance that we knew everything about him. *We felt compelled to complete our memory of him.*

We also strongly felt that an apology for how events *had evolved* would have gone a long way to helping us accept what had happened. We were not asking for any admission of liability for what had happened, but a simple apology would have helped us both. Of course, no one was prepared to do this, although each individual involved seemed to convey the impression that the standard of care had not been as it *should have been*, but it was not *their* fault, but *someone else's.*

We felt that we had been *collectively* failed, and that each step of my pregnancy and labour, and Gregory's birth, had consequently led on to the next step, leading to a catalogue of errors which had *spiralled beyond all control.*

There was also another reason for us needing to find out what had happened. Without any understanding of this, how would we in the future be able to make an informed choice as to whether or not we should try for other children?

The following year was taken up with writing so many letters and meeting with so many officials on so many occasions that it became one of the most exhausting times of our lives; also serving to heighten the grief we were feeling at the loss of our only child.

Deciding that we would have to be very proactive if we were to obtain answers to the overwhelming number of questions which had now begun to emerge, we threw all our energies into ensuring that Gregory's birth and death should not simply be swept under the carpet. We were both strongly of the opinion that it was our *right* as parents to have our questions answered.

I telephoned Mr Winterton at the House of Commons, and to his credit he took my call, instead of leaving a secretary to deal with it. After speaking with him at some length, and after he had studied a copy of the letter of complaint I had forwarded to Macclesfield, he decided that as MP for the district where the hospital was situated that he should pursue shortfalls in the maternity services on offer there.

I also discussed our situation with the Macclesfield Community Health Council, and a lady called Trish Johnson, the Chief Officer for the Council, was helpful in clarifying our thoughts so that we could compose a list of questions which we felt needed answering. All these questions were sent to Macclesfield so that all the individuals involved would have time to prepare answers.

Months sped by with numerous phone calls and letters passing to and fro, but we became no clearer to an understanding of what exactly had happened and why, than we had had on the day of Gregory's birth. This was a time of terrible grief as we both questioned *everything*.

Was there a *genetic cause* for Gregory's abnormality, was it something either of us had *done*, or *omitted* to do in preparing for the pregnancy? Had we inadvertently *exposed* Gregory to something which had caused his spina bifida? I recall desperately emptying kitchen cupboards and staring at the labels of cleaning products there, almost as though expecting to read a warning about the dangers of spina bifida on one of the labels. Ross considered all the chemicals that he had worked with prior to the pregnancy, but we could come up with no answers.

The situation seemed unbearable. Not only had our son died, but we couldn't seem to get any answers to the most basic of our questions concerning *how* or *why* he had died.

This inability to obtain information led us to even more questions. We now questioned whether medical staff were being evasive because they had something to hide, or whether they were so concerned that we would sue that they had decided that the best attitude was to tell us as little as possible so that they should not be found lacking or liable in any way. This evasiveness led us to now question whether Gregory had died *because* he had spina bifida or whether he had been *damaged* during labour or birth. Although when Gregory had died, we had strongly felt that we didn't want his body tampered with as it had been throughout all his short life, we now felt that if there had been a post mortem that this would have answered a lot of our questions.

We didn't know where to turn to obtain answers to all the questions which had emerged.

Eventually, a meeting was organised at the hospital and we met with *some* of the staff who had been involved with our care, some administrators – including Mr Jaycock the Unit General Manager, and a lady called Dr M Spencely – Director to Public Health, who spoke on behalf of the obstetrician, who had now become so hostile, seeming unused to having to explain herself, that she not only refused to answer any of our questions, but also refused to shake our hands at the outset of the meeting. The paediatrician did not attend.

As we wished to speak to her also, a subsequent meeting had to be arranged for us to do this. We came away from *both* these meetings with little better an understanding than we went into them with.

One concession was made in the first meeting, and that was that in the week leading up to labour it was agreed that I *had been* unwell. I had read that there can be a problem called *hydramnios* – which means that there is an excess of amniotic fluid – associated with babies who have spina bifida. I asked whether it was thought that I had been suffering with this as all the signs seemed to indicate that I had been. Mrs Scott, the obstetrician, did interject here, pointing out that this condition does not usually produce any symptoms, and seemed sufficiently annoyed with me for daring to suggest this as a diagnosis, that she blurted out that my symptoms were 'compatible with pre eclamptic toxaemia.'

We were both saddened by how the meetings had gone, and resolved that we needed to do something positive to ensure that what had happened to us didn't happen to someone else. *Obviously, the exact same scenario would be unlikely to ever happen again, but any one aspect of it could cause us more hurt than words can explain.*

As more time elapsed and we had no greater an understanding of what had happened than at the outset, both Mr Hamilton and Mr Winterton wrote to us to ask whether we wanted to have our situation referred to the National Health Service Commissioner. Deciding to pursue every avenue open to us to obtain information we agreed that we did, and Mr Hamilton, our MP, undertook to contact the Commissioner on our behalf.

The days passed slowly and we became not only frustrated by the passing of so much time but despondent too. We decided that we should ask to see both my medical notes and Gregory's, thinking that perhaps *this* would shed some light on the situation. Consequently, Mr Hamilton again wrote on our behalf to Virginia Bottomley, the Secretary of State at the Department of Health, to request this. Her Under Secretary, Roger Freeman, replied on her behalf in a letter dated 30 April 1990 which read:

'Dear Neil,

Thank you for your letter of 2 April to Virginia Bottomley on behalf of Mrs Francesca Nield of ..., Knutsford about her obstetric notes.

I am sorry that Mrs Nield is not satisfied with the service she has received. Medical staff make records to enable them to treat and care for patients for as long as necessary. A consultant holds a patient's medical records on behalf of the health authority which controls the hospital concerned. Whether a patient or her GP can have access to the record will be decided by the health authority and consultant between them. This is a matter in which, among other considerations, the consultant's professional standards on confidentiality must be respected. It is not one in which the Secretary of State would wish to interfere.

I hope this explanation is helpful.'

This was followed on 6 June 1990 by a letter from William Reid, the Health Service Commissioner, to Mr Hamilton, which he forwarded to us. It was a lengthy letter, typed with single spacing covering two A4 pages.

The gist of the letter explained that 'some aspects of the complaint are, in principle, within my jurisdiction, and I might be able to investigate them; but some of Ms Nield's major concerns are, I am afraid not open to me.'

The letter went on:

'As you know my work is governed by the provisions of the National Health Service Act 1977 (the Act) – which are outlined in lay terms in the enclosed leaflet. Paragraph 19(1) of Schedule 13 to the Act (section 4(b) of the leaflet provides that I shall not investigate action taken in connection with the diagnosis of illness or the care or treatment of a patient, being action which, in my opinion, was taken solely in consequence of the exercise of clinical judgment. This means that I could not look into any possible shortcomings in the diagnosis of Gregory's condition or the clinical management of his, and his mother's care. You will see from section 5 of the leaflet that there is a special procedure which can sometimes be used for complaints about the clinical judgment of hospital medical staff, and further information will be available from Mr Jaycock, the Unit General Manager at the Hospital, if your constituent wishes to consider that option. However, I cannot say whether Ms Nield's case will be appropriate for review under that procedure.

I see from the papers that Ms Nield alleges negligence on the part of certain members of the hospital staff. Negligence is a matter for the courts to decide – it is not for me. Moreover section 116(1) (b) of the Act provides that I shall not investigate any action in respect of which the person aggrieved has or had a remedy by way of proceedings in any court of law. This is explained in section 4(a) of the leaflet. If I were asked to consider further the possibility of an

213

investigation, I would need to know whether or not Ms Nield was intending to take action against the Health Authority or any member of their staff in respect of any aspect of her complaint. You will also see from section 5 of the leaflet that the special procedure to which I referred earlier cannot normally be used where an individual wishes to seek a legal remedy for a complaint.

I can look into complaints about failures in service or maladministration by health authorities. Therefore, I could in principle, take up Ms Nield's grievances about the attitude of the technician who carried out the scan on 9 June; the alleged exchanges between a midwife and Dr Oliver on 22 November when an attempt was made to attach a fetal scalp electrode – but for the reason I have previously explained, I could not question their clinical (professional) competence; and the alleged insensitivity and lack of information after the delivery by caesarean section. Even if I were to investigate and uphold any part of Ms Nield's complaint – and this might not be my position, I could not cause the Health Authority to discipline any member of their staff or make individual's give personal apologies.'

The letter went on:
'Your constituent may conclude that I would not be able to conduct a sufficiently wide investigation to satisfy her, but I shall gladly consider the case again if I am provided with all the background papers, a clear statement of the

aspects of the complaint Ms Nield wishes me to look into together with an assurance that she is not intending to take legal action. This should be done as soon as possible to avoid a lapse in time which can cause an investigation to be fruitless. ...'

It concluded:

'I regret that I cannot be of more help at this stage. ...'

As I finished reading the letter, my heart sank. I already felt that the lapse of time which had occurred since making the complaint had led to *any* investigation now being fruitless. However, as I *so* strongly felt that we had *not* received an *adequate* standard of medical care, and that the only way to ensure that any changes would be implemented to ensure that *some* improvements might be made, was to pursue every avenue available to do this, so we decided to move on to the next step of the complaints procedure indicated by the letter from the Health Service Commissioner and request an Independent Professional Review.

Dr Simpson, the Regional Medical Officer for Mersey Regional Health Authority agreed that if we assured him that we were not contemplating taking legal action that the Health Authority would proceed with a review. With this in mind the Health Service Commissioner decided that, 'the IPR may prove to be a better forum in which Ms Nield can give voice to some of her concerns.' Consequently, he decided that it would be inappropriate for him to now proceed with our complaints. In a further letter to Mr Hamilton, again forwarded by him to us, he stated:

'If Ms Nield finds that the IPR does not include any substantial issues which nevertheless fall within my jurisdiction, then I shall be very pleased to consider her case again, if she (or you on her behalf) will send me the correspondence which arises. This should be done promptly – once the IPR has been held – to avoid the lapse in time which can make an investigation fruitless.'

Although we were advised by Dr Simpson that: 'The consultants for the review are chosen by the Joint Consultants Committee as experts in the field under consideration who have no personal involvement or allegiance with the staff, hospital or district under review.'; and also that: 'Every effort is therefore made to ensure their independence.', we were not given any indication as to when the review would be undertaken and were also unhappy with the idea of the profession assessing its own members. This hardly constituted *independence* in our minds.

It was 26 July 1990 when the letter from the Health Authority finally arrived, stating:

'Dear Ms Nield
I have now heard from the Joint Consultants' Committee that Mr. P.Donnai, consultant Obstetrician and Gynaecologist of St.

Mary's Hospital, Manchester, and Dr. P.D.Edwards, Consultant Paediatrician, Princess of Wales Hospital, Bridgend, Glamorgan, will be acting as assessors in the Independent Professional Review.

Mr. Bernard Morgan will be contacting you shortly to fix a mutually convenient date for the Review to take place.'

We were to become more and more frustrated as *months* passed with us pressing for the Review to be held as quickly as possible and having now to deal with yet another bureaucrat who had been assigned to deal with it. It was 17 August when Mr Morgan advised that: 'My difficulty at the moment is getting future dates from the independent consultants because of their present absence on annual leave.'

Eventually we were given a date for the Review. It was to take place on 1 November 1990. This would mean that almost a year had passed, during which time we had been offered no information from the medical practitioners who had looked after me and Gregory as to what had gone wrong with my ante natal care, labour, and Gregory's care.

It was during the summer that I became aware of the fact that a lady in Macclesfield was involved in joint legal action against the Mersey Regional Health Authority and the Manchester Health Authority on behalf of her son, who had been born some years earlier with spina bifida. She had been under the care of Mrs Scott initially at Macclesfield, and then transferred to St Mary's, Manchester, where she had been under the care of Mr Donnai, the expert who was to sit on our Independent Professional Review.

I spoke to this lady, and also to her solicitor - Mr J M Kitchingman from Pannone Blackburn Solicitors based in Deansgate, Manchester - and we spent an afternoon in his office exchanging information on both our situations. I realised with dismay the length of time, and stress, not to mention cost, which this family had had to go through to ensure that medical mistakes which had been made concerning their son were heard in court.

Although we had no desire to pursue a court case ourselves - although if Gregory had lived I feel that we might have had no option but to do so, as a buffer against the costs of all the special care he would have undoubtedly needed – we were angry about how all avenues for redress seemed to be stacked against us.

In anger, I again wrote to Mr Simpson calling into question the independence of Mr Donnai - the expert who had been chosen to conduct the Review - in the light of what we had learned about the joint legal action being taken against him and Mrs Scott. He passed no comment on this and the Review went ahead with Mr Donnai acting as the independent expert. It wasn't until the following year, on 12 March 1991, that Mr Simpson responded on this matter.

'The Health Authority were not involved in the selection of the Independent Consultants. This is done by the Secretary of the Joint Consultants

Committee in London who take steps to ensure the independence of the Consultant view.'

On a positive note, Mr Kitchingman did point us in the direction of an organisation called AVMA - which stands for 'Action for Victims of Medical Accidents,' a registered charity founded in 1982 to assist patients who become victims of medical accidents or who feel that they have not been properly cared for - and a lawyer for this organisation, named Leslie Keegan, looked into our case for us.

His approach was compassionate, but considered and pragmatic. We were both grateful that he took the time to consider our situation in depth. I reproduce the main points he made in a lengthy letter directly to us. The quotes are reproduced as written.

'Firstly, may I say that I am extremely sorry to see that both you and your husband have had such a dreadful experience your account of events is extremely thorough and it portrays not only a disgraceful and harrowing series of events but also the deep sadness which you both feel over the death of Gregory.

... Thus, it would appear that the alpha-fetoprotein test was not carried out too early.

With respect to the ultrasound scans it would appear that expert opinion is needed as to whether an open lesion should have been detected either on the occasion of the first scan (9th June 1989) or the second scan (26th September 1989). However, expert opinion would also be needed as to whether the symptoms that you presented together with the family history would have indicated that a higher resolution scan should have been carried out.

Legal Aspects

Now, speaking purely on the legal aspects of the case it would appear that there are certain aspects which indicate that the standard of care you received may have fallen below an acceptable level. The acceptable standard of care is that which was first set out by NAIRN J. in BLAM v FRIERN HOSPITAL MANAGEMENT COMMITTEE. and it is that of the ordinary skilled man exercising and professing to have that particular skill.

Thus in the case of the technicians the standard expected would be that of the ordinary skilled technicians intthe [sic] case of the obstetrician it would be that of the ordinary skilled obstetrician and so on.

The legal issues would be mostly concerned with the issue of whether the presence of spina bifida could/should have been detected by the level of scan carried out or whether it would have been appropriate to carry out a higher level scan i.e. one with higher resolution involving the use of more sophisticated equipment and more highly trained personnel.

...

In law to establish negligence it is necessary to establish 3 things: (1) That the Plaintiff (Patient) was owed a duty of care (2) that there was a breach of that duty of care (3) that damage was caused to the Plaintiff by that breach of duty of care.

Thus it would appear that there may have been a breach of the duty of care owed to both yourself and Gregory but nevertheless the 'damage' was not caused by this breach of the duty of care because from the account which you have supplied it appears that he would probably have died in any event. Thus this particular point would not appear to me to found a claim of negligence. Of course, it is only necessary to establish that there was one breach of the duty of care and that this caused damage to establish negligence. In this case it appears to me that the stronger point would be that because the level of care and/or skill employed by those requesting and/or those carrying out the scans that an open lesion of the spinal cord was not detected. However, it may well be that the independent medical expert will disagree with this point.

Damages

I know that before I expand on this point that you will say that you are not interested in monetary compensation. However, it is a point which is of some importance because it has to be weighed in the balance against the costs of bringing an action.

221

I am afraid that the general view of the law is that to award damages for the death of a child would be a highly speculative exercise and so there is only a minimal amount which a person may recover for the death of a child. This is referred to as bereavement damages and amount to some £3,500. Thus, if it could be shown that because you received an inappropriate level of care antinataly [sic] or during the birth or because Gregory was not properly attended to after the birth that Gregory died then this is the level of damages that would be awarded.

If it could be shown that because the scans were not carried out appropriately that you were deprived of the opportunity of having a termination of pregnancy and that because of this you were subject to the heartbreak of seeing your child born suffering with spina bifida and then seeing him pass away then you will also recover some damage. If also yyou [sic] suffered some form of post-traumatic stress, which is defined as some form of recognisable psychiatric illness or disorder (e.g. depression) then you are likely to recover damages for this also. The level of damages would depend on the impact which the incident had on your life. Thus, for instance, if it has meant that you have been unable to work then obviously the damages would be much higher than otherwise.

As I said above, I fully realise from your letters and documents that it is accountability and assurances which you want and not damages because quite clearly nothing could compensate your [sic] for the awful experiences that you had.

Turning then to other aspects of the case. I am enclosing details of how to initiate a complaint to the GMC. I am also enclosing details of how to initiate a complaint about Nurse(s).

I have also enclosed full details of how the GMC investigate a complaint. From the account which you have given me it would appear that there are grounds for making complalints [sic] to these bodies.'

The letter continued at some length, outlining the procedure for litigation and costs. We were very grateful to Leslie Keegan for the work he undertook on our case - which was undertaken free of charge - but, perhaps more importantly, he helped to clarify our thoughts, and although he was pragmatic he was also very compassionate.

We decided not to follow the advice in his letter about making complaints to the GMC. We were by this time exhausted by our numerous, and seemingly fruitless requests for information. Also, it seemed pointless to seek retribution for attitudes and mistakes which could not now be changed; we knew that we would have to live with what had happened. We had also by this time become cynical about the medical profession assessing itself, and so decided that it would be fruitless to follow this route. Instead, we decided to await the Independent

Professional Review to see whether this would shed any light on how and why everything had gone so wrong.

All that we wanted was a full and honest explanation of this and also an apology. Although we were prepared to await the findings of the Review, we didn't particularly hold out any great hopes for this.

Compassion

As Ross showed the undertakers out, I stared at the black cardboard box which they had placed in front of me on the coffee table. When Ross returned, his face grey, furrowed with sadness, he removed the lid with trembling fingers. Inside was a simple plastic bag, into the corner of which Gregory's ashes had settled; both the bag and the box incongruous in size to its contents. The sprinkling of grey and white dust bore no semblance to my thoughts of Gregory, and I turned on my heel and left the room.

After a day or two we decided that we should buy a more attractive container for the ashes, and when we had purchased this – a tiny urn with a delicately traced pattern in green and gold with a detachable lid, we placed them in a smaller bag inside it.

Immediately after Gregory's death Ross had expressed the desire to scatter his remains on Kinder, a mountain in the county of my birth – Derbyshire, which we had climbed together many times. Recalling our many treks up there; when always even on the sunniest of mornings as we set off, the weather would inevitably close in as we approached the summit. There, heavy clouds would menace, soaking our faces; a whipping wind always adding insult to injury. I shuddered at recollections of this, remembering how this wind was so forceful that it would sting our faces, so that we would have to huddle together in a crevice between rocks to even catch our breath.

I decided that I could not bear the thought of Gregory's ashes being blown around the bleak, inhospitable mountainside.

Unable to think of an appropriate place to scatter them, nor a permanent place of important significance to us where we could place them, we put them on a shelf in the box room - which served as an office for us both; which is where they remain to this day.

The more we procrastinated about what we should do with them, the harder it became to do anything with them. Now, it is my wish that when I die that they should be mingled together with my ashes: mother and child reunited forever. This now seems so appropriate and gives me comfort.

But in those desperate early days there seemed nothing we could do to ease our pain; there seemed no place that we could go, no activity which could distract us from our terrible grief. It was all pervasive, enveloping us; trapping us in a deep, dark well of despair. We could hardly breathe as it threatened to suffocate; its force sapping us of energy, and yet continually tormenting so that we could scarcely rest or sleep.

We visited St Cross Church in Knutsford, whose minister had so kindly conducted Gregory's funeral but we found no comfort there. My thoughts constantly returned to Booth Hall Children's Hospital as this was where we had spent our time with Gregory, and I felt a deep yearning to return there.

With this in mind, we wrote to Miss Carys

Bannister, the neurosurgeon who had looked after Gregory to ask if we could do this. We were nervous about contacting her, feeling that she would scarcely have time to talk to us; her role as an eminent world-renowned consultant neurosurgeon surely meaning that she would be too busy. To our surprise she welcomed our visit and set aside several hours for us to talk with her on a Saturday morning.

It was overwhelming to return to the ward where Gregory had been nursed; and this time as we stood in front of the notice board, upon which were pinned the numerous photographs of children with all manner of dreadful illnesses, which had so horrified us previously, today, we proudly added a picture of our son.

We were nervous as once again we were shown to the office where we had talked to Miss Bannister and her staff on the morning of the day Gregory was taken off life support. We didn't have long to wait before she appeared. We were concerned that she shouldn't think that we were questioning her involvement or skill in Gregory's care, but were so desperate for information - *any* information which could be provided to fill in the gaps in our knowledge about Gregory, so we were bursting with questions to ask her.

Her demeanour was calm as she listened carefully to our questions. She showed no sign of sitting in judgment of the questions we asked, which may not have been questions which she might have expected; and she showed no signs of impatience or defensiveness, her responses delivered calmly and considerately, in what immediately became apparent to us both was an honest way. If there was anything which we didn't understand she was careful to rephrase it so that we as laymen should understand it. She answered all our questions at length repeating herself where necessary, or rephrasing something which we didn't immediately understand.

It was difficult to know where to begin; we had so many questions, but we started by asking why the causes of death had been listed as they were on the death certificate. We were at this time wondering whether Gregory had died *because* of his spina bifida, or whether he had *also* been brain damaged, either during labour, birth, or afterwards. She replied that what had been listed on the death certificate were the legal requirements, and the events which had been part of the process of his death.

She explained to us that he had had the most serious type of spina bifida and we asked if he had lived what sort of life he might have expected. She was completely honest in her response, telling us that he would have been paralysed and thus wheelchair bound, that he would have been incontinent, with poor mental functioning and visual problems.

At this point I asked about Gregory's eyes. Their colour had puzzled me. The only time I had seen him with his eyes open was when he had been taken off life support and lay in Ross's arms dying. I was surprised to see his eyes fly open and seem to gaze directly at Ross's face. They were the most beautiful but darkest eyes I had ever seen; and believing that all newborn babies have blue eyes I asked whether this was because he had spina bifida. I felt tears stinging the backs of my own eyes as she confirmed that he had had the most beautiful dark eyes; indeed had been a beautiful baby.

We conversed for some time then about how much pain and discomfort he would have felt during his short life, and she told us that she felt that he would have felt pain or discomfort from the operations, but that it wasn't thought that life support causes pain; although obviously she could not be certain of this.

She told us more about the operation to insert the shunt to help with the hydrocephalus which Gregory had been suffering from, and told us that Gregory's shunt had been into his abdomen.

We also discussed how upset we were about how events had unfolded during the latter stages of pregnancy, labour and afterwards, and she responded that doctors in such circumstances also get upset too. She told us that Dr Shackleton had been very upset when she had talked to Miss Bannister on the day that Gregory had been born and transferred from Macclesfield to Booth Hall Children's Hospital; also mentioning that the anaesthetist who had been in attendance at the Saturday morning meeting when it had been decided to take Gregory off life support had also been very upset. He was due to move into working in intensive care and had questioned his ability to cope. I thought back to the sobs and noises of noses being blown in the office that morning, and thought that it must almost be as difficult for the staff as the parents to deal with such situations.

Before leaving, we discussed the prospects of us having further children, and she advised us to see a geneticist to discuss this before making any decisions; recommending Dr Dian Donnai, a consultant clinical geneticist, based at St Mary's Hospital for women and children in Manchester. I told her that not wishing to return to Macclesfield for a post natal check that I had instead attended a different hospital for this - Wythenshawe Hospital, and that the consultant I had seen there had already written a referral letter on our behalf to Dr Donnai.

She gently told us that we could conceive another baby with spina bifida, but that we could also conceive a healthy baby. She explained that if we did try for another child that the pregnancy would be very carefully monitored with higher resolution scans and amniocentesis if we wanted these tests. She also mentioned that we should discuss the idea of me taking a folic acid supplement with the geneticist before getting pregnant, as research seemed to be indicating that mothers who did so were less likely to conceive another baby with a neural tube defect. We discussed the research which was being undertaken on neural tube defects; and she informed us that research was going on worldwide, with a lot of money being spent on it in America.

We lingered in the corridor not knowing what further to say. Placing her hand upon my arm she suggested that we talk to other parents who had lost children, to try to share our grief; and even, if possible, to try to find some *creative* way through it. She told us that some parents who had lost children had told her that they found comfort in writing poems or painting; and she recommended that I should read the author Susan Hill, who had lost a child, and had written a novel about loss.

Her final words before parting lodged in my mind, that writing about our experience, might not only help us, but might help others if shared. Encouraged by her kindness, and by her advice about sharing our grief, we joined a local group called SANDS, an acronym for the words 'Stillbirth and Neonatal Death Society' and talked to others who had lost young children. Although I didn't mind talking about Gregory's death, Ross was uncomfortable about doing so with this group of people, who were effectively strangers to us. It was also difficult because each child's death had been different, and we felt so overwhelmed by how events had transpired for us that it was difficult to articulate this to the group.

Recalling Miss Bannister's words, I sat down and wrote an account of Gregory's death, reproduced here in Appendix 1. I tried to write in a positive way, but it only conveyed a modicum of what I was feeling. This account was published by SANDS, ASBAH, 'Association of Spina Bifida and Hydrocephalus' and in a booklet entitled *Brief Lives*, published by the NCT, the 'National Childbirth Trust.' Details of these and other organisations can be found in Appendix 2.

There were very few books written by parents about the death of a child, but I read all those I could find and empathising with the bereaved parents, I felt slightly less alone. Always an avid reader, from being a small child I could lose myself in words. Although grief had robbed me of my enjoyment in reading fiction, I read anything and everything factual which I felt would help me in my understanding; and help on my dark journey back to normality.

I questioned how *nature* could be so awesome and also so cruel. Having always enjoyed walking and gardening, I would often marvel at its many wonders; perhaps watching a gelatinous blob of frogspawn in a pond become wriggling tadpoles and then hopping frogs, caterpillars changing into spectacularly marked and coloured butterflies which could fly on tissue-thin fragile wings, observing perhaps the tenacity with which a wild flower could grow from a rock seemingly deplete of both sunshine and the nourishment of any soil; while noting how the ferocity of its strength could create such dreadful havoc: gales uprooting trees which had stood firm for hundreds of years in a matter of moments, or lightning ripping through the sky, sending its dangerous electrical discharge spiralling indiscriminately from clouds to the ground.

It was at this time that I came across a poem by William Wordsworth, a long poem written in eleven stanzas which had taken two years to write. It is known as 'Intimations of Immortality,' although its full title is, 'Intimations of Immortality from Recollections of Early Childhood.' Wordsworth writes about nature, trying to understand it, to reconcile the loss of his childhood vision of it. It is a complex poem where he mourns the loss of his childhood innocence and vision which he describes at the outset as:

'THERE was a time when meadow, grove, and stream,
The earth and every common sight,
To me did seem
Apparell'd in celestial light,
...'

The poem describes his struggle to retain a relationship with nature through memory, and he describes his struggle to see through mortality to a soul that is immortal. He explains how his mature mind eventually enables him to love nature and all natural things; reconciling himself to the loss of his childhood vision. In the tenth stanza he writes:

' ...
What though the radiance which was once so bright
Be now for ever taken from my sight,
Though nothing can bring back the hour
Of splendour in the grass, of glory in the flower;
We will grieve not, rather find
Strength in what remains behind;
In the primal sympathy
Which having been must ever be;
In the soothing thoughts that spring
Out of human suffering;
In the faith that looks through death,
In years that bring the philosophic mind.'

I learnt these words off by heart, and they became my mantra whenever thoughts of what had happened to Gregory threatened to overwhelm me. I thought at length about the complexity of nature, and marvelled that so many babies are born healthy given the complexity of creation. *He ends the poem on words which had I not had and lost Gregory I would not understand*:

' ...
Thanks to the human heart by which we live,
Thanks to its tenderness, its joys, and fears,
To me the meanest flower that blows can give
Thoughts that do often lie too deep for tears.'

The Dales Way

Locking the door behind us, leaving the car on the drive, we set off on foot for the railway station. Not even pausing to look back at the house, we headed for town.

It was a warm, damp day in June, the wet path giving off slim snaking vapours of steam, drying quickly; and I felt overdressed in all the layers I was wearing.

Although physically uncomfortable, my legs leaden, feet heavy inside sturdy walking boots, a feeling of relief overtook the numbness which I had felt as Ross had made preparations for the holiday. It swept over me like a huge wave; and I felt as though I didn't care if I was never to return home again.

The sweet scent from roses lining the path, released by a battering of large, warm raindrops, wafted into my nostrils, in a physical way: a physicality I had previously enjoyed about nature, but which had been lost to me in previous months.

They had been so tortuous, with such intense grief, that I felt as though I had almost become devoid of feeling. Everything that I had previously cared for had become as nothing.Today, as my nostrils twitched with this sweet scent I felt a smidgeon of emotional relief.

The raindrops splashed the roses like teardrops, bruising the delicate petals. I noticed some buds were still tightly closed with browning petals, which I knew would die on the stems without opening; and a name sprang sadly into my mind: *Gregory*. This was followed by the words:

'... the meanest flower that blows can give
Thoughts that do often lie too deep for tears.'

Now, instead of carrying an emotional burden, I carried a rucksack upon my back, containing everything I needed for the week. My face was bare of make-up, my hair tied loosely back. I felt more liberated than I had for months.

The rucksack contained everything I was going to need: clean underwear, socks, a couple of t-shirts, a comb, a waterproof cagoule and over-trousers. I wore the jumper instead of carrying it, but took this off immediately as it was so warm, tying it loosely around my waist.

The previous months had left me feeling so vulnerable, stripped of all dignity; and it felt good to be leaving everything behind, even my beloved garden.

I had paid little attention to the arrangements Ross had spent the last few months making, being so absorbed in grief. For months he had pored over maps, studied guide books, made telephone calls and written letters. And, finally, his plans were now coming to fruition.

He had made arrangements for us to walk The Dales Way, a recreational walk designated for ramblers by the Countryside Commission as a medium distance footpath: a route which connects two National Parks, passing through the beautiful countryside of the Yorkshire Dales into the scenic Lake District. It is an 81 mile trek from Ilkley, situated at the edge of the West Yorkshire conurbation, through the heart of the Dales, and then on to Bowness in the Lake District. He had split the walk into sections and pre-booked accommodation for each night; so that we had a destination to aim for each day.

As the old train rattled and shook its way towards Yorkshire; curled into the corner of a heavy fabric seat, stiff with layers of dirt and scabbed with dark shiny patches of aged chewing gum, my head resting against a grimy window which rattled alarmingly in its wooden frame - in time with the laboured mechanical clang and wheeze of the train, my thoughts strayed to events of the previous months.

So much seemed to have happened, in such a short space of time.

The hazy reflection of my face, scarcely visible through the multi-layered smudges of dirt glistening on the glass in the sunshine, seemed unrecognisable to me. It was as though a stranger peered back.

I thought about how events had not just turned our lives upside down, but how they had affected others too. The expression I had seen on great aunt Jenny's face on the day of the funeral could now be the one reflected back at *me* in the dirty glass.

My face had become strained and hollow, and my frame had lost all the weight I had put on during pregnancy.

I was taking a medication, called Pregnavite Forte F - a vitamin supplement given to women who have conceived a child with a neural tube

237

defect, on the advice of a genetic counsellor, even though we hadn't as yet decided whether we were going to try for more children.

Since Gregory's death, we both strongly felt that although we didn't want to go through the same experience, or anything similar, that having had a child - albeit for such a short time, had enhanced our lives, which seemed very empty now.

I reflected ironically that the vitamin supplement at least ought to help me get through the walk.

We had visited the genetic counselling clinic at St Mary's Hospital for women and children in Manchester in April, and had been seen there by Dr Dian Donnai, a consultant geneticist; who had taken our details and assessed the risk of us having another child with a neural tube defect. She gave us a pamphlet devised by the department of Medical Genetics, which outlined information about neural tube defects, and methods currently available for diagnosing them ante natally.

Having had an affected baby, she informed us that we would be entitled to more close screening than previously, with amniocentesis and detailed fetal anomaly scans being offered to determine the health of any subsequent babies.

All this information was whirling around inside my head as the train took on more momentum as we entered Yorkshire, my eyes straining to see the countryside, passing in a distorted blur of different shades of green as I squinted against the sunshine, now searing persistently in stronger rays through the dirty glass.

As I strained to see a seemingly endless blur of patchwork fields, broken only by grey drystone walls, I began to feel a headache coming on.

I sat upright in my seat and closed my eyes. The image of a beautiful baby came into my mind. As easily as ever tears sprang to my eyes, and I quickly brushed these away with the back of my hand, hoping that Ross had not seen them.

He was preoccupied with studying a map, and I was glad that he at least had something else to occupy his mind. I tried to nap, but before we knew it the train was pulling into a station.

We spent the night in a guest house in Ilkley, where once in our room I studied the map for the first time, and noted with some alarm the route which Ross had planned.

It was a relief to escape into the fresh air the following morning, finding the room that we had been allocated cramped and claustrophobic. It was very clean, with an en-suite bathroom, but was overwhelmingly peach, in colour and accessories; including a highly-scented bowl of pot pourri and air freshener in the bathroom. We escaped that evening to a pub for a meal.

The bed had nylon sheets, and we spent the night sleeping on top of the covers with the window open as wide as it would go. The following morning, we gulped in the clean Yorkshire air, swallowing it in huge, greedy gulps; pleased to be out of the over-sanitised, deodorised rooms.

Shortly, we were again assaulted by strongly fragranced smells. This time they were more natural scents, from assorted plants on sale at a Garden Centre we rather bizarrely had to pass through to begin the walk.

Although it was early in the day, and it was only just opening for business, the sun was already strong enough to crush the different smells from leaves and flowers, which wafted through the air on a gentle breeze. Some were sweet as perfume, others so bitingly sharp that I could taste their acidity on my tongue. I felt a small surge of excitement as we made our way past the plants set out on trestle tables, some still tightly packed together in wooden crates, seeing a signpost marking the beginning of 'The Dales Way.'

We crossed an old stone bridge straddling the river Wharfe, heading for Bolton Abbey. From there we intended to walk to Appletreewick, where Ross had booked accommodation for the night in a pub.

As we walked, the sun came out, so we removed our sweaters, putting them into our rucksacks. We were silent as we began the walk, focusing only on placing one foot in front of the other; probably both thinking about how far we had to go. We walked at a steady pace, the gentle lowland path boasting exquisite scenery.

From time to time we stopped for a breather, or to take a photograph. Sometimes we had to stop because the scenery was so breathtakingly beautiful: the river gurgling over rocks, spitting ice-white bubbles, tree branches idly dangling into the water; fish slinking quietly in the safety of bottle-green and grey shadows cast by the trees.

We passed a large garden with a couple of peacocks standing majestically in the centre of a neat lawn. We paused for a moment to watch the ornate birds. They stood proudly, with heads upright, wearing crests on their heads, almost like crowns; their long trains resting on the ground.

We watched in awe as one of the birds fanned out its tail. Although we had seen this so many times before, it was as spectacular as ever as we watched the feathers splay out into an iridescent blue-green plumage, the intricate eye prints within the feathers seeming to watch us in return. Although marvelling at the complexity of the structure, span and colouring of the feathers, I thought about how their long trains must hamper their movements and possibly cause some distress to the birds.

Shaking our heads at the complexity of nature, we continued on our way.

As we approached Bolton Abbey, looking forward to eating the sandwiches we had been provided with at the guest house, a heavy downpour emerged from nowhere. Fumbling in our rucksacks we hastily put on our waterproofs. Through a sheet of rain, we could just make out magnificent skeletal ruins of the Abbey.

The old Augustinian priory seen from this distance, with surrounding meadows and sweep of the river, created an idyllic scene. We were disappointed that it was raining so that we couldn't get any good photos. Today there were a lot of visitors about, either wandering through the largely intact shell of the priory, or picnicking by the river. As the rain became heavier, and showed no sign of stopping, most had hastily gathered up their things to seek shelter.

As the downpour continued, we spent only a short time wandering through the ruins, deciding to continue walking rather than eating our sandwiches in the rain. After pausing to study a guide book, we headed off through woods following the river Wharfe, to an area known as 'the Strid.'

As we plunged deeper into the woods the river became narrower, eventually emerging as only a very narrow channel.

The scenery at the Strid was unlike anything I had seen before. Although the river becomes the narrowest of channels at this point, the water is exceptionally deep, and the area very dangerous; many having drowned trying to jump across what seems to be a very narrow span to the other side of the bank. Today, the water thundered so loudly that our voices were deafened by its roar.

Clambering carefully across grassy rocks and massive uneven slippy boulders, made smooth by the pressure of the water over the years, we saw holes and fissures so large that a person could easily fall through them; to be swept away into the numerous chasms and tunnels, many hidden amongst the huge boulders, to be sucked into one of the many whirlpools there: whose swirling waters spat out globs of water which ran down our faces.

Pausing for a moment to refer to the guide book, I read about the many deaths that have taken place at the Strid; and about a local legend which recounts how a white horse appears in the area if someone is to die there.

I felt a surge of panic as Ross continued clambering from boulder to boulder peering into the deep chasms. Looking from him, then down at the swirling vortex beneath the boulder upon which I stood, I began to feel dizzy. Glancing up, I studied part of the river where the water rises in a sheet of white spray, creating a high waterfall which crashes down over a huge boulder into the river; and imagined that it would be easy to visualise this sheet of water as a huge white horse, rearing high on its two back legs before its front hooves come crashing down.

It was a relief to continue safely on our way, eating our sandwiches on a bench on a more secure footpath. Behind us, in the hedgerows, tall mauve foxgloves stood stately and erect like sentries on duty. The air was dank with heavy scents of wet vegetation and steam as it grew warmer again. Although the rain had eased, dark clouds scudded across a grey sky.

The weather all afternoon was variable, sharp downpours lowering the temperature, alternating with spells of warm sunshine; so we both shivered and broke out in beads of sweat, pulling our waterproofs on and off.

Before leaving the low footpath which follows the course of the river, we paused to admire the arc of a rainbow which appeared, dipping from the sky into the river; a multi coloured rippling spectrum surfacing the water.

We now took a path which wound its way up a steep slope towards Appletreewick; situated off Lower Wharfedale. We left the lowland path of the Dales Way scrambling up to the village where we were to stay for the night.

Occasionally, blinded by the rain, I stumbled on roots of trees growing up through this lesser-used path; perhaps a shortcut created by the locals from the village to the river, slipping on ferns which had been trampled underfoot, and scratching myself on brambles lining the path, protruding in all directions from overgrown hedges; occasionally pausing to eat the plump, juicy blackberries which weighed down the brambles, staining our fingers inky blue.

As we struggled against the denser vegetation, the weather took a turn for the worse, and it began to rain very heavily. Although the lush vegetation formed a natural canopy of sorts, large drops of water dripped through the overgrown, entangled greenery to wet us through. I began to feel cold as water dripped down my neck, putting up the hood of my cagoule, but it seeped through even the tiniest of gaps. We walked more quickly now, hoping that it wouldn't be too long before we reached our destination.

When we did eventually make it to the top of the steep slope, we paused on flat ground to recover our breath before beginning to look for the pub where Ross had booked a room.

A mist had descended as we had climbed and visibility was poor. Eventually, with a feeling of relief, we saw the outline of a building loom from the mist, and we knew from grid references on the map that this should be where the pub was.

This feeling quickly turned to panic as the pub sign swung wildly in a wind which was quickly gathering momentum; and with no lights to be seen coming from inside, and its situation from the way we had approached it making the pub seem desolate - or indeed abandoned - my heart skipped a beat.

We banged on the heavy wooden door to no response. We walked around the pub and thought that we could see a dim light upstairs, so once again returned to the main door, which we continued to bang on intermittently until our knuckles became sore.

Eventually, a light came on and we heard the noise of bolts being slid open and a key turning in the lock. The innkeeper peered out, squinting into the darkness, asking us who we were and what we wanted. Ross reminded him that we had a room booked for the night, and he stepped to one side to allow us to enter. As we took off our wet outer garments I noticed the landlord watching us.

Shivering with cold, with our clothes soaked through to the skin, we squelched through the pub in our wet socks, carrying our muddy boots, cagoules, over-trousers and rucksacks. The landlord led us to a guest room upstairs. Once there, he leered at me as he said,

'You will catch your death unless you get out of those wet clothes.'

He punched the mattress of the wide bed, and jokingly pronounced that he would be happy to join us to help get me warm as there was enough room in the bed for three; and if I went in the middle, I would soon get warm.

Whether he meant this as a joke or was drawing our attention to the comfort of the wide bed Ross grinned as he said this, but shaking with cold I didn't find it very amusing and shot him the dirtiest look I could, not in the mood for any kind of banter.

At dinner downstairs that night I avoided him, although watching him chatting amiably to his customers in the well lit and warm pub I felt that I had probably misjudged him. It is probably a reflection of my mood at that time, that on returning to the room, the door of which had no lock, I wedged a chair under its handle. I quickly fell into a deep and, *for the first time in months*, unbroken, and peaceful sleep.

At breakfast I again avoided the landlord, although in the stark light of a new day he looked even more harmless. Chatting to Ross he told him that the locals didn't call the village 'Appletreewick,' but rather referred to it in local dialect as 'Aptrick.'

After a good breakfast I was now eager to once more set off walking. Today we were heading to Grassington, the capital of Upper Wharfedale, at the southern tip of the Yorkshire Dales, for lunch.

Although a fine drizzle fell as we set off, as the morning passed the weather began to improve; the sky changing from grey-pink to dull white, then the subtlest shade of washed blue, before a blazing sun burned away all the heavy clouds, turning it azure blue.

We ambled along the beautiful riverside

path, my mood lifting with the weather, crossing quaint stone bridges and passing hamlets with chocolate-box picture cottages. We crossed through farmers' fields, where cows and sheep grazed unperturbed in the sunshine, opening and closing gates secured by anything from rusty wire to old thick greasy rope. Buttercups lifted their bright yellow chins to be tickled by the sun.

We crossed stiles of all types and climbed over ladder stiles; also passing at regular intervals through kissing gates. As we passed through the first kissing gate Ross stopped inside it and planted a kiss on my lips. I noticed that for the first time in months he was smiling, and his brow seemed less furrowed than previously. For the whole of the remainder of the walk we kissed at every kissing gate.

Grassington bustled with activity and noise, a strange contrast to the quiet of the morning where we had only come across one or two other ramblers. It took some time to find somewhere to eat, the cobbled market square swarming with people. It was a pretty village, obviously very popular with tourists; beautiful stone cottages, with climbing plants clinging to the stonework, pots and troughs and hanging baskets making the village awash with colour.

We were to regret spending the amount of time we did over our pub lunch as the afternoon had left us with a lot of miles to cover if we were to get to Buckden before dark. We followed a path which climbed above the valley, opening onto a flat, wide plateau paved with limestone.

It was easy and pleasant walking on this

247

open, flat terrain, the grass grazed so short by sheep that it seemed like a carpet underfoot, interspersed with huge, invariably flat, limestone rocks. It was as though a lawn had been laid for a giant, with the flat limestone rocks a stepping stone path.

We dawdled, enjoying the springy grass, littered with large solid black pellets excreted by plump sheep, enjoying the afternoon sun; exploring coves or a cairn. Pausing to study the map, we realised that we needed to pick up our pace if we were to get to our destination before nightfall.

It was with regret then that on entering the beautiful setting of Kettlewell village that we had no time to spare to take in the sights. With longing we passed tearooms and cafes advertising cream teas.

As we put the miles behind us, it was surprising how the only thought for both of us now was to get a meal that night. The longer we walked for the more hungry we became. My spirits soared as I spotted a village in the distance, only to be dashed when we found by studying the map that this was a village called Starbotton.

On approach to this village we saw several National Trust volunteers, busy repairing drystone walls. Mopping wet brows across the backs of hands, they tried to engage us in conversation, but we could only pause for a few minutes, telling them we were heading to Buckden for the night.

Eventually, we arrived here, the name of the village meaning 'valley of the bucks,' as it had once been a hunting area. It was as though we were on a hunting mission ourselves now; we were so desperate to get our next meal. Stripped of all other responsibilities this necessity to eat became all-important. Also, the physical exercise had given us an appetite which we hadn't had for months.

The cottage we stayed in was tiny but very attractive, and after a quick shower, we headed off to an inn marked on the map. Fortunately, not only did it serve food, but it served very good food and we enjoyed one of the nicest meals of the holiday. We went to bed that night feeling well fed and relaxed.

The following day was sunny and we luxuriated in the lushness of the countryside as we walked. Today, I felt overwhelmed by its fecundity. Everywhere I looked seemed to be swollen with fertility; with vegetation and crops in abundance, and wild plants, ferns and creepers spilling over onto grass awash with wild flowers.

I breathed deeply, taking in the heady scent of wild honeysuckle, and thought that this must be the best scent in the world. The grass looked tender and sweet, every cow with its head down tearing out mouthfuls of it, even though their overfilled udders seemed to be straining under the weight.

There were rabbits everywhere, and although they scurried away when we got close, they were happy to scamper on the path ahead, or in the grass to the side of us; obviously breeding baby rabbits by the dozen if the number of them was anything to go by.

I thought about Gregory. Watching the rabbits enjoying the sunshine; for the first time as I thought of my son, I didn't feel as sad as previously, but rather marvelled at nature in all its splendour. I lifted my face up to the sun and let its rays gently caress it. For a moment, *I lived in that moment*, and was happy to feel the warmth from the sun soak deep into my skin, warming me from outside to within.

Although I knew that this feeling would not last, I was pleased to experience it. If I had felt happy for a moment in the sunshine, I understood that I could *still* experience happiness; and that the future was slightly less bleak than I had thought it would be over the past few months.

I understood then that although the journey would be a long one, it was a journey worth making; that one way or another it would end with me regaining some normality.

Little did I know how short-lived this feeling would be.

For now, I was grateful to enjoy the early morning sunshine; ambling through beautiful meadows, watching the bobbing tails of rabbits scampering in the sunshine, the sun warm and comforting.

I am glad that I didn't know how the rest of the day would evolve.

From Buckden, the Dales Way follows the river Wharfe to its source on Cam Fell. This is the most difficult part of the route, as it involves a climb to its highest point of 1,699 ft over open moorland. It is probably as well that that morning I had no idea how difficult I would find this.

The beautiful meadows gradually began to give way to rougher grasses; then peaty mud, then even rougher terrain. As we climbed, I could feel the scar from my caesarean section, feeling as though it was being stretched; and I developed pain across my stomach and a stitch in both my sides.

As we headed for the limestone crags at the summit, I began to feel as though I was wading through treacle in Wellingtons which were too large for my feet. In reality, my walking boots sank with seemingly every footstep into boggy mud. The ground was sodden, but covered with bog moss it was impossible to assess how firm it was just by sight.

Step after step sucked us into deep sticky mud. To make things worse the mud squelched over and into my boots, so that my socks became wet and sticky, making my feet feel even heavier.

As we climbed, the cloud cover made it difficult to see very far ahead, and the mist began to soak through our hats and gloves. We were wearing cagoules and waterproof trousers, but the exertion of the climb made me break out in beads of sweat inside the protective clothing.

It was then that I felt Gregory's loss as keenly as when he had first died.

With tears and droplets of mist rolling down my cheeks, and the moisture seeping up through the ground, it seemed as though the whole countryside was weeping in unison for my loss; and I felt as though I couldn't take another step.

Unfortunately, there was no choice. We

were stuck on this mountain, with no-one else around, and it would have been as difficult to go back as it was to move forward. This seemed to sum up where life had led us.

Physically, I felt then as though my whole body was crying, and that these tears of despair were being echoed back at me by the habitat.

I was completely disinterested in any of the wild flowers or birds we might have expected to see. Blinded by emotion, I saw no sign of the golden plovers, merlin or grouse we might have spotted. My ears were deaf to the warbling songs of skylarks, which should have been distinctive here. The wind and my emotions muffled the plaintive piping of the golden plovers which inhabit this upland moorland in the summer.

As the wind whistled, stinging our eyes as it swept across the moor, it felt like the most inhospitable place on earth. It now became as much as we could do to stay on the correct path; knowing that in such weather conditions that it would be easy to wander from the path, and to fall into one of the numerous and deceptively deep pools here covered in blanket moss.

Eventually as we got higher, the mist lingered in patches beneath us, with visibility improving a little. We removed our waterproofs, laying them out to dry on a limestone boulder. The terrain was as bleak as it was lonely; with no other human or building visible.

It was a relief to reach the summit.

As the path became wider and drier, it became easier to walk upon. We were to be further cheered to see a signpost marking the point where the Dales Way meets the Pennine

Way. Seeing this landmark raised our spirits after labouring for miles with no sign of anything but the steep path ahead; although I made a mental note not to agree to walk this more difficult footpath should Ross suggest this in the future!

We descended Cam Fell without seeing any other ramblers, surprising as it was the beginning of summer. Occasionally we caught a glimpse of a building on the horizon, perhaps an old barn or a remote farmhouse. The rain and mist still hung as heavy as my thoughts; but knowing that we were growing ever closer to our destination for the night gave me added momentum to carry on, knowing that we were slowly but surely moving closer to shelter, and physical comfort - in the form of a shower or bath, and a meal.

Tonight we were booked into a cottage where we would be provided with a meal, and the thought of someone else taking responsibility for this was very comforting. All we had to do now was to find the cottage.

Studying the map, we noted that this was situated several miles beyond the fell but before the village of Dent; where the trail follows the river Dee along Dentdale. Realising that we still had a way to go, we slowed our pace as each step took us out of the mist into a dull grey, but drier, atmosphere.

It was a relief to get off the fell even though it was a grey afternoon; and we idled a while now, investigating a cave we found and crossing Gayle Beck. As we approached a remote farm - the first sign of civilisation we had encountered for several hours, a small blur of white with glimpses of brown, bounded past us, before backtracking, coming to an abrupt halt in front of us.

A terrier, perhaps a Jack Russell, which couldn't have been more than 12 inches high jumped at each of us in turn, its round hard padded feet leaving muddy footprints on our jeans. It had a short stubby tail and pressed its face into our legs. Its small but strong jaw barked a deep greeting.

As we pushed the dog off it leapt in mid-air, showing us how acrobatic it was, its almond shaped dark eyes full of life and very expressive. Unable to resist the intelligence which seemed to radiate from its eyes we patted the small dog, who in reward entertained us once more by showing off its prowess in jumping and climbing. It bounded towards a tree, and to our amusement hit the tree head on with the full weight of its body, before rebounding from the sturdy trunk. It was fearless as it energetically chased birds, or invisible flies, with no hope of catching them. It ran, jumped wildly, foraged and dug in the hedgerows, seemingly all for our amusement. We laughed at its antics.

Moving on, the dog followed us. Several times Ross led it back to the farm, but each time he returned, it appeared behind him. Eventually it grew more cunning, as we at last thought that we had shaken it off; only for it to appear once more at our side. We were now so far away from the farm where we had first encountered the dog that we were reluctant to return with it.

Despite the fact that we persistently shooed

it away, we found that it would not return home. Deciding to ignore it in the hope that it would grow bored and return home had *no* effect. It was treating our meeting as a game now; and although it often retreated a good distance away, sometimes several hundreds of yards, we still caught glimpses over the next hours of its almond eyes or small thick ears protruding from a ditch or hedge where it was hiding.

Although concerned that the dog was now so far from home that it would be lost; having walked so far we were unprepared to return to the farmhouse with it.

Our attention was eventually diverted from the small dog by a massive stone viaduct at Dent Head. Part of the Settle-Carlisle railway, the high viaduct, consisting of ten arches and constructed from blue limestone, is an impressive sight: its construction a prodigious feat of Victorian civil engineering. It could be seen from miles away, and although man-made it seemed to fit into the landscape without spoiling its appearance, but rather enhancing it.

As we approached the viaduct we were astounded by how high and long it was. We were on a road now which led to the cottage where we would be staying the night; and we felt dwarfed by the blue legs of the limestone arches, rising to 100 feet in height, its ten arches spanning 199 yards.

We had a couple of miles to walk to the cottage, and tired, we fell silent, our footsteps falling in unison. Too tired to talk to each other, the silence of the remote countryside was only broken by the yapping of the terrier which was still following us, or our occasional, weary, verbal efforts to shoo it away.

As dusk fell early, helped perhaps by the mature trees which lined both sides of the road; whose branches stretched the width of the road, so that they created a green tunnel overhead, through which only the occasional chink of light filtered, we heard the sound of a car engine in the distance.

As it grew louder, we looked behind us to see a Landrover approaching, its headlights on; the dark, damp road glistening in their beam. As it drew alongside us it stopped. A woman with a headscarf covering her hair was behind the wheel, and she reached into the back to open the door on our side without speaking. Thinking that she was offering us a lift, we were surprised when the terrier leapt in a blur of white and brown from its hiding place in the hedge onto the back seat of the car. Its tail wagged with glee, as it took up its position on a blanket laid out on the seat. Resting its head on its front paws, its beautiful almond eyes closed immediately in sleep.

Pausing only for long enough to tell us that her dog frequently followed ramblers who passed the farm, she quickly and adeptly turned the Landrover in the narrow road, leaving us to make our weary way to the cottage.

The cottage was difficult to find in the growing dark; situated in the middle of nowhere. Eventually we came upon it, nestling in a valley. A cobbled path wound its way between long coarse grasses filled with wild flowers to either side of the path. This led to a rickety wooden porch, from which flaked white paint. No attempt had been made to tame the garden, so the grass was like an ungrazed meadow; in fact the only evidence of the cottage looking occupied were dim lights coming from within, and a hanging basket swinging in a gentle evening breeze beneath a dim lantern over the porch.

We were so tired and hungry now, that I feel that I could have eaten anything, and slept anywhere. An old lady with a shock of white hair led us through a tiny sitting room, cluttered with books and newspapers and old well-used and faded furniture, to a very steep set of stairs.

She showed us to our room, which was very basic, and then led us to the bathroom. An old cast iron bath took centre stage. There was no shower and no mains water; although she told us that there should be just enough hot water for four of us to take a bath, informing us that another couple who were walking the Dales Way would also be staying that night. She told us that when we had finished bathing that we should go down to the sitting room for our meal. Before leaving, she warned that we should not be alarmed by the colour of the water, which would be brown from sediment in the water tank, and not to fill the bath too much as the supply of hot water had to go between us all.

I lowered myself into the couple of inches of water I had allowed for my bath, and despite the fact that it was indeed brown in colour, I have never been so grateful to take a bath as I was that night. As the mud and sweat from my body mixed with the brown dregs of water, I felt the heat of it penetrate all my aching joints.

We were introduced to the other walkers over a glass of wine in the sitting room as our host prepared the meal. We exchanged information on the walk, and discovered that this older couple from Wiltshire had taken a day's break in the middle of the walk; which had refreshed them, and, more importantly, given their feet a rest – the man was suffering badly with blisters on his feet. Ross and I had been lucky not to have suffered too much rubbing of our feet, although my boots were now beginning to look shot.

This couple told us about their route and where they had spent their nights, and we discovered that we would both be spending the eve of the final day's walk at the same farmhouse in Cumbria. We talked about meeting there again, and decided that if we all successfully completed the route that we would go out together for a celebratory meal in Bowness-on-Windermere, which was the end of the walk.

Our host was unobtrusive, but very hospitable. Although her cottage and her cooking were simple, it was the most homely of the places we had stayed in throughout the walk. For dinner she served a simple tomato and basil salad with a home made dressing, and then lamb with home grown potatoes and vegetables. The meal was finished with a delicious apple crumble and custard. I was surprised by my appetite, woofing down everything she laid in front of me.

Retiring to bed, the mattress was lumpy and the springs squealed with every movement, and I thought that it would take some time to fall asleep. It was extremely dark in the cottage, but the next thing I became aware of was the call of a cockerel. This woke me up, followed by a loud thundering noise on the roof. I couldn't imagine what this might be. It was so loud that I didn't think that it was a bird, feeling that a bird would be incapable of making such a din. I listened carefully for a moment and now heard a tapping against the window. Getting out of bed, I flung back the curtains and peered through the rickety old sash window - curtained by strands of ivy which were causing the tapping, to the sight of a beautiful blue sky; the sun already drying the dew on the grasses beneath the window.

Once again, at breakfast our host was very hospitable, although in the natural light of day the simplicity and threadbare nature of our surroundings was more apparent. As we left the cottage, I paused at the top of the cobbled path and looked back. I was startled to see a goat on the roof. The cottage was in a cleft in a valley - which was level with the hill surrounding it; and the goat walked freely from the hill onto the roof of the cottage. It became clear what the noise had been that I had heard earlier that morning. It was a goat walking on the roof!

Something about this scene created a whole different way of thinking for me. It wasn't that I had an apocalyptic moment; but rather that my thoughts changed, in a subtle way initially, but definitely in a groundbreaking way. From that day on, *I began to think differently.*

Where previously I had thought that life followed a natural order, and consequently was devastated when Gregory had died, I now came to realise that there was *no such order* in the world.

Looking at this cottage, everything about it was ramshackle and higgledy-piggledy. I couldn't help but think that however much we might tend to our houses, and our lifestyles; however much perhaps a farmer might care for his livestock, that we are all in a sense fighting *against* nature all the time.

I became aware of a fundamental truth – and that is, that ultimately nature will always *have its way.*

The cottage exemplified this truth. I noticed that nature already seemed halfway to reclaiming it; observing creepers clutching at its skeleton, causing cracks in its walls, while weeds pushed up everywhere, even in the roof. The hills and trees seemed to be hemming it in, pushing against its very structure; spiders seemed to own a good proportion of it, as there were cobwebs everywhere. Slime from slugs and snails hung in repellent trails on the filigree mould covering the cottage. To cap it all, there was a goat eating the tufts of grass and weeds which sprang from the roof. It surely couldn't be long before nature reclaimed the cottage as her own.

And I realised that this was what happened to all of us eventually, and that there was no stopping it, however hard we might try. We all have an indefinite time on earth, and when

260

nature beckons for our return, there is nothing within our power that we can do to avoid it.

From the cottage we followed the river Dee to the remote village of Dent. This morning I noticed a subtle change in habitat. Although Dent lies within the Yorkshire Dales National Park, it is actually in Cumbria; and we noticed tell-tale signs of this, one of which is that the fields were now bordered by hedges instead of walls. As it was early in the day and the weather was good, we decided to explore the village. It felt like we were stepping back in time as we meandered through its narrow cobbled streets, admiring its medieval church and old cottages, many of which were painted white. I was later to read that this white-washing is a Cumbrian tradition.

We couldn't resist spending some time in this charming village, and enjoyed ourselves sightseeing and taking photographs. We were attracted by a large granite monument in the centre of the village. Cool spring water flowed into a trough at the bottom of the monument, and cupping our hands we drank mouthfuls of this refreshing clear water. The monument was a tribute to someone called Adam Sedgwick, whose name was etched into the granite, followed by the dates, 1785-1873. We took some photographs of this, and I made a mental note to research this man on our return home.

After lunch in an old inn in the village, we set off that afternoon for the market town of Sedbergh. Studying the map we noticed that this nestles below the steep slopes of the Howgill Fells, which create a bridge between the

Pennines and the Cumbrian mountains. Despite being in Cumbria the smooth, grassy, rounded slopes form the north-western fringes of the Yorkshire Dales.

It didn't appear to be a difficult or unduly long walk, certainly nothing like the walk over Cam Fell, so I was surprised that Ross seemed to be in a hurry to get there.

As we approached the town, entering on a high footpath alongside a wind-swept golf course, the heavens opened, and not having time to get out our waterproofs we quickly became soaked. As I studied the dark sky, noticing how the darkness and the contours of the Howgills created a dramatic backdrop to the town, I was glad that we had reached the town as the heavens opened; rather than getting drenched earlier.

I was not unduly concerned about being so wet until I asked Ross where we were staying that night; feeling that it couldn't be far away, and that it wouldn't be long before we could get out of our wet clothes and into a warm bath or shower.

It was then that he told me that he had had some difficulty booking accommodation in the town from home, and had decided that as it was a largish town with a couple of pubs that he had felt that we ought to find some accommodation for one night relatively easily on the day we arrived.

As his words trailed away on a wind which was growing stronger by the minute, we both hastily fished in our rucksacks for our waterproofs at the same time, without speaking.

No words were exchanged on our walk into the town. As we squelched along in our wet clothes beneath the waterproofs we avoided eye contact.

We enquired at all the inns and guest houses we came across, and there were many in this market town; but there was no accommodation to be had anywhere. Beginning to panic now at the thought of having to sleep under a hedge or in a bus shelter, we bought a drink at the last pub we tried and sat at a table with it trying to determine what to do.

It was one of the other customers, a local, who on overhearing our plight, suggested that we enquire at the Tourist Information Centre in the town, pointing us in its direction, telling us that we should get our skates on as it would be closing for the day soon.

This we duly did, and after many phone calls the lady on duty there managed to secure us some accommodation for the night at a bed and breakfast on the outskirts of town. It was quite a long trek to the guesthouse, but eventually we arrived at a large semi-detached house set back from the road by a long, immaculately kept garden. The lawn was as pristine as a bowling green. In fact, it looked as though every blade of grass had been hand-cut to the same length by a pair of scissors.

We were ushered to the side door by the lady owner, who had been pre-warned by the Tourist Information Centre of our arrival. Immaculately dressed and made-up, and with not a hair out of place, we noticed how she seemed to be making an enormous effort to prevent her nostrils from twitching with disdain at the sight of us.

Making some comment about what a state we were in, she asked us to strip off as many clothes as we could, leaving them in an outhouse, along with our boots and rucksacks, only taking into the house the bare essentials we needed. Showing us to a room I got the distinct impression that she would really rather we had remained in the outhouse.

Once in our room, almost a replica of the one we had stayed in in Ilkley; over-cluttered with figurines and smelling highly of air freshener, she surveyed her room with loving and concerned eyes. It was almost as though she couldn't bear the thought of letting us use her beloved room, and rushing off told us that she would send up her husband to show us where the bathroom was.

When he appeared, as we had so few clothes on, I remained in the room while Ross went with him to the bathroom. On his return, Ross threw himself down on the bed, complaining about all the rules and regulations he had been issued with by this man on the use of the bathroom. He let me take first shower, warning me as I scurried across the landing with only a towel for modesty not to let the shower curtain fall outside of the bath, nor to step onto the bathmat until I had towelled myself almost dry, promising that he would perform the rest of the chores in the bathroom *as instructed* after he had showered.

Once showered, we returned to the outhouse to collect our clothes and headed back to a pub in town for a meal, pausing only for long enough to notice the numerous paintings and photographs cluttering the walls of the landings and stairs of the guesthouse.

In the pub we got talking to a man who was sitting alone eating dinner, who introduced himself as Sam. On overhearing our conversation about how we were walking the Dales Way, an older man and his son at a table nearby joined in the conversation, informing us that they too were walking the route. As we chatted we found that coincidentally we were also all staying in the same guest house for bed and breakfast.

Fortunately, we discovered that we had all been greeted in the same manner; concluding that possibly this couple didn't enjoy having paying guests in their home, but perhaps were having to do it to earn a living. We all stayed out as late as possible, leaving as many of our possessions as we could in the outhouse, before creeping up the stairs to our respective rooms in our stocking-feet. After a few drinks, none of us found it easy to do this *quietly*, and it was all I could do to stifle my giggles.

Once in our room, Ross and I fell back on our bed and let the giggles come. Helped by the drink, the giggles turned to laughter, which then turned to guffaws. As tears of laughter fell down our cheeks, tiredness eventually overcame us, and throwing off the few clothes we had on, we quickly fell into a deep sleep.

I think that we were all as sheepish as each other as we entered the dining room for breakfast the following morning. A round table had been set so that we might all eat breakfast together. With none of us daring to make eye contact, we exchanged a few pleasant civilities about the weather and our plans for the day.

It was here that the hostess came into her own, fussing around, introducing us all to each other, not knowing that we had already met in the pub the previous evening. Her *pièce de résistance* caused us all great amusement, as Sam, the lone walker, asked for more toast. He nearly choked on his bacon and eggs as he watched the hostess twirl an empty toast rack in her hands, telling us that she had had the bright idea of using this as a container for a flower arrangement at her next flower arranging class. After all, it would signify her love of her job as a guest house owner; and her 'delight' at meeting her visitors! Once he had managed to swallow the mouthful of food he had almost choked on, Sam gazed at her open-mouthed!

We fell over each other in our attempts to finish breakfast, to pay for our stay, and to get away from the house as quickly as possible. We made it a few yards down the road; hopefully out of sight of the house, before howling with laughter.

Not having laughed for so long it was good to do this: and we perhaps laughed more than the situation warranted, our laughter only subsiding when we developed stitches in our sides.

At Sedbergh, the Dales Way leaves the Yorkshire Dales, and as we walked that day I began to think of our far we had come. The scenery had changed; and now instead of following riverside paths and passing tiny villages set in valleys, we crossed meadow after meadow, all full of wild flowers, and walked across rolling farmland.

There were many farms scattered along the way and crossing through their yards, felt it an intrusion if we met with the owners or any of the farmhands: noting rusting machinery; or hay and manure swept hastily into heaps, which took our breath away, steaming in sweet ripe vapours beneath the heat of the sun.

Sometimes the meadows were knee deep in grass and had so many wild flowers that they attracted clouds of butterflies which flitted from flower to flower. Other fields burst with crops; in others sheep grazed.

Everywhere was alive with the sweet scents and noises of summer.

The air hummed with the noise of insects. As bees and insects buzzed and hummed, and cows swished their tails to swat flies which were irritating them, we gradually began to become aware of a droning noise which didn't sound natural. It didn't sound like a tractor or other farm machinery, but the noise was constant. Although seemingly distant, it became louder as we continued to walk.

As we were at a loss to determine what it was, we paused to study the map for clues. We decided that it must be the noise of the M6 motorway, the sounds of which, although still a long way away, must have been carried on the still air. When we eventually crossed a bridge over the motorway we did so quickly, disappointed to see all the cars speeding in both directions. I thought about how quiet and calming the last few days had been; devoid of noise and speed, and realised how healing this had felt.

Long after we had crossed the bridge, my spirits felt low as I thought about how we would soon be returning home, to normality; or to the normality we had come to know, with all the difficulties that this would entail.

It was Friday, and tomorrow we would complete the walk, before returning home by coach on Sunday.

From being completely disinterested in the holiday at the outset, I now felt sad that it was nearing an end, wondering if I would again sink into terrible depths of grief on our return home. I didn't enjoy the rest of the afternoon; dwelling on the return home and the difficult decisions we would have to make once there.

We spent that night in a remote farmhouse, enjoying watching the skill of the young farmer's son as he directed his sheepdog to round up the sheep. We had venison steaks for our evening meal. At first I wasn't sure what to make of them; never having eaten deer before, and feeling queasy about eating it, but although I found the texture of the meat quite dry, it was lean, and I thought that its flavour was not dissimilar to beef.

We were up early for our final day, which would be a relatively easy walk to our final destination of Bowness-on-Windermere. We had met with the couple from Wiltshire at the farm, but decided to complete the final stage of the walk alone, promising to meet up for a celebratory meal at the conclusion of the route.

We took our time today, trying to make the most of the beautiful rural Cumbrian countryside; but the day seemed tinged with sadness for us both. We strayed from the route to make the most of our final opportunities of the holiday. We wandered through forests, splashed in streams, and sought out tarns.

The tarns were an irresistible draw. The map was littered with these small bodies of water. It was a bright sunny day, and the tarns we found reflected water which was brilliant blue; choked with plants such as pondweed, duckweed, sedge and iris, which attracted so much wildlife that it was difficult to know where to look first. This dilemma was solved as brilliantly coloured iridescent dragonflies, flying on shiny wings attacked us, with the stealth of bomber planes, so that we had to focus all our attention on avoiding these.

Reluctantly, we finally had to proceed on our way, and eventually the mountains of the Lake District came into view. Their peaks were so high that they merged with the clouds, creating a dramatic backdrop to the picturesque scenery around us.

For me, it was almost as though they signified a barrier. Boldly crowning the horizon, they signalled the end of our journey.

It was almost an anti-climax then to reach the signpost at journeys end; where a tourist kindly took our photograph for us as a memento of what we had achieved.

Completing our Memories of Gregory

It would not be true to say that our walking holiday resolved our grief. What it achieved for *me* was a different perspective on it. It was difficult to return home and to once again enter the empty nursery, and I wept as deeply as when Gregory had first died when I saw the tiny urn containing his ashes. When I wasn't working, I wandered from room to room of the house, not knowing what to do with myself.

Although we had received genetic counselling, we did not discuss whether or not we should try for another baby. In fact, we spoke very little about the future, seeming to have a tacit understanding that we would have another child, but that whatever happened was in the hands of fate and beyond our control; although I was careful to take the Pregnavite Forte F vitamin supplement as advised.

I researched this and discovered that some specialists working in the field of genetics did not feel that there was sufficient folic acid in this supplement, so I wrote to one of these – Professor K M Laurence, from the Institute of Medical Genetics at the University Of Wales College of Medicine.

He very kindly replied to my letters; also sending me some research papers about the occurrences and nature of spina bifida, and information on supplementation with folic acid in an effort to reduce such occurrences. After writing to Dr Dian Donnai, the geneticist we had originally seen at St Mary's Hospital in Manchester, and visiting a dietician there, I decided to take extra folic acid as a precaution should I become pregnant.

It was a busy time, with numerous letters still passing backwards and forwards between us and various officials as we continued in our attempts to discover why events had occurred as they had, and to fill in the gaps in our knowledge of everything that had happened to Gregory.

We now had a date for the Independent Professional Review, which was to take place on the 1st November, and I hoped that this might provide us with more information.

All we could do now was to wait.

Once the photographs of our holiday had been developed, prompted by the photograph of the monument hewn from the huge slab of granite in Dent, which commemorated the life of Adam Sedgwick; out of idle curiosity I decided to see if I could find any information about this man.

I discovered that he was the son of a Cumbrian vicar who had been educated at Cambridge. There he had gone on to pursue a distinguished career as a Professor of Geology, making a name for himself as the father of modern geology, shaping nineteenth century ideas on geology and palaeontology. I also read that he was a devout Christian.

It was while I was reading about his religious beliefs that I noted that Darwin had been one of his pupils. Charles Darwin had started his career studying medicine at

Edinburgh University, but repelled by anatomy and surgery had in 1827 been sent to Cambridge to study Theology instead.

At first Sedgwick and Darwin shared religious views, not doubting the literal truth of the Bible, and believing that every species was created through divine decree; and had remained fixed since creation.

Where Sedgwick remained staunch in his views, Darwin's belief dwindled. It was in 1837 that he reached the momentous conclusion that species evolved, or originated by descent with modification from other species. He believed that they were neither fixed nor created by miracles.

His scepticism, which strongly challenged the widely-held Victorian religious beliefs of that time, was strengthened in 1851 by the death of his daughter, Annie, at ten years old. Initially fearful of upsetting Christians who held such strong religious beliefs; fearing that his evolutionary theories would not only create controversy, but would result in him being deemed an *atheist*, he was reluctant to make his thoughts public. It wasn't until 1859 that he published his famous book, *On the Origin of Species by Means of Natural Selection*.

He explained that after the death of Annie, he came to regard pain and suffering as a result of general laws, rather than there being any direct intervention by God. He pointed out that *he* didn't regard himself as an atheist; he didn't *deny* the existence of a God, *but rather regarded himself as an agnostic*.

I thought back to how I had felt when

Gregory had died, and although not professing to have anything like the brilliant mind of Darwin, I understood how confused his thoughts would be after losing his daughter; his grief and beliefs compounded by his research.

Reading about Darwin made me even more frustrated about aspects of Gregory's illness and life which I did not understand. Had he died because he had spina bifida, or had he also been damaged by medical incompetence? The numerous letters passing back and forth were not answering any of our questions about this.

We decided to once again approach Miss Bannister, the neurosurgeon who had cared for Gregory, as she had been so kind in previously answering our questions, to see if we could obtain any further information from her.

I explained to her that as we had had so little time with our son, that we felt we wanted to know *everything* about him, and told her of the difficulties we were encountering in our attempts to find accurate information about his problems.

She explained that when she had first met Gregory at Booth Hall Children's Hospital that he was in a very poor condition; in fact in such a poor condition that he wasn't taken for a brain scan, but instead scanning equipment had been taken to the ward to him, as it was obvious how poorly he was.

She told us that staff accompanying Gregory to the hospital had informed her that they had had to ask for the ambulance to pull over at one point on the journey to Booth Hall from Macclesfield as they had *lost* him in the

273

ambulance; and had had to resuscitate and reintubate him in the ambulance at the side of the road. This they had undertaken with great difficulty.

He had been diagnosed by the paediatrician when she finally discovered his spina bifida before he left Macclesfield as having a 'myelomeningocele', the most severe form of spina bifida; which diagnosis Miss Bannister confirmed as correct. She explained that the paediatrician had not diagnosed hydrocephalus, but that this isn't easy to diagnose, and that at that time Gregory had shown no outward signs of suffering from this. She went on to explain how hydrocephalus often leads to poor mental functioning.

She explained to us that babies with such severe spina bifida as Gregory had often die at birth. He had what is known as an Arnold Chiari II malformation. This is an abnormality of the cerebellum; where the back portion of the brain is displaced from the back of the skull down into the upper neck. Hydrocephalus occurs because the displaced cerebellum interferes with the normal flow of the cerebrospinal fluid, whose purpose is to nourish the brain and spinal cord. The interference of the flow of cerebral spinal fluid to and from the brain leads to the accumulation of cerebral spinal fluid in the empty spaces of the spine and brain.

Presented with a patient in such poor condition as Gregory, she talked about the conversation which she had had with Ross and his parents on the morning of Gregory's birth, whilst I was in hospital at Macclesfield. She then answered all our questions about the two operations that she had performed on Gregory - to close the spina bifida on his back and to insert a shunt, and was completely honest in her opinion that if Gregory was ever to breathe that he should have done so after the operation to insert the shunt. The fact that he hadn't reinforced how damaged he was.

I don't know how Ross felt as he listened, but I felt that what she was telling me was something which I had *instinctively* known since Gregory's birth, but nonetheless, *I needed* EVERYTHING *spelling out for me*. I needed to be sure that Gregory's respiratory problems were caused by the spina bifida, and that he had not been damaged during labour or birth. She explained that they had occurred because of the spina bifida, and added that she didn't believe that he could swallow. As she mentioned this, I felt that this could explain some of the problems I had suffered with at the end of my pregnancy, and why I had had so much amniotic fluid.

I felt numb, and we all fell silent for a while.

Miss Bannister left us to our thoughts; neither encouraging us to speak, nor making us feel uncomfortable for taking up her time.

Eventually, I asked whether Gregory's problems could or should have been spotted on the scans. She replied that they could or should have been, because Gregory's bone structure was damaged. I recalled seeing Gregory at Macclesfield after his birth, and had seen for myself his damaged spine, with bone and other bloodied matter so clearly visible to me even through a haze of anaesthetic.

She told us that Gregory's spina bifida was an open lesion and that all that she had been able to do that day was to perform an operation to cover this, so that it should not become infected, and insert a shunt. We then discussed why it had been missed on the AFP test, and she reinforced what we had discovered for ourselves; that this test has to be performed at an exact point in the pregnancy, and that even then the success rate for the test is not high.

I felt angry that I had been completely misinformed when I had booked into clinic about the success rate of the AFP test and scan complementing each other in determining such problems.

I told her of my fear that Gregory's head had elongated on the Saturday before we had taken him off life support. She replied gently that it had.

I thought then about the time he had spent on the ventilator; about how it had given us time to get to know Gregory, but also reflected on everything he had been put through, and the cruelty of him having been ventilated when he had had no hope of independent life.

Presented with Gregory in the condition he had been brought to her, I understood the dilemma which Miss Bannister would have had to face. We talked about this, and she told me that experienced doctors do not take these situations lightly, but also get very upset.

This led on to a conversation about the difficulties of ventilation. I told her how awful - and guilty, I had felt on that Saturday morning when I had asked for Gregory to be taken off ventilation, and that he be allowed to die with peace and dignity in our arms. Here, she was very compassionate, taking my hand and telling us that if there had been *any hope* for Gregory that the doctors would not have agreed to the request.

Tears ran down both mine and Ross's face as she told us that we had made a brave decision, and that it was a decision borne from love because we cared about our son.

She told us then of a conference that she had recently attended [in Spain if my jottings are accurate] where a doctor had presented a paper concerning the ventilation of babies in a similar situation to Gregory; in effect those who were stillborn. This doctor had been involved in an experiment where eight such babies had been kept alive on ventilators - to see what would happen to them, but that each had died at varying stages from ventilation-related problems. She told us that this paper had not been well received by the other delegates at the conference; and that she had mentioned Gregory's situation, hoping that we wouldn't mind her telling her colleagues of this.

On the contrary, we felt that it revealed her respect for life.

All this information was too much to take in at once; and leaving the hospital after the meeting I felt every bit as upset as the day we had left Gregory behind there after his death. As I cried and raged at the bleak grey sky, a slither of light, or perhaps it was a teardrop, came into my vision. For a moment my thoughts lost their heaviness. I gazed at the cloudless bleak sky and

277

the general greyness all around me - *and questioned whether this was all there is?*

I couldn't answer, but it certainly felt as though life was now a struggle against darkness, with only an occasional glimpse of light breaking through. Despite my religious upbringing; like Darwin before me, I felt that although I wasn't an atheist that I would never be able to follow any religion, nor forget what we had seen Gregory suffer. I knew that I would now always be an agnostic.

Recalling Gregory's appearance in my bedroom in the form of light and wings after he had died, I felt that there had to be some other, as yet *inexplicable*, aspects to life; but I felt that any answers would not come through religion.

As we returned home, the overwhelming feeling which emerged for us both was a deep feeling of gratitude towards Miss Bannister.

She had completed our memories of Gregory, and we remain eternally grateful to her for this.

Independent Professional Review

There seemed little point in holding the Independent Professional Review. It was now almost a year since Gregory had been born and died and we didn't see how anything could come of this review so long after the event.

We were satisfied that Miss Bannister had answered all the questions which had perplexed us for so long, but decided that it would be rude not to attend the review as arrangements for this meeting had already been put into place.

We had also waited such a long time for this.

We had been asked to allow a full day for the review as a schedule had been organised which involved Dr P Donnai, acting in his capacity as a consultant obstetrician, and Dr P D Edwards, a consultant paediatrician, interviewing doctors who had been involved with our care, and these independent experts discussing our concerns with us; following which they would compose a report on the situation.

It was raining heavily when we arrived at Macclesfield hospital, and I felt indifferent to the surroundings, and the doctors we passed in the corridors as we all moved back and to the same room at different times to be *interviewed* about what had taken place. Dr Donnai was a thin man, who fidgeted with his spectacles, with Dr Edwards, who as I recall had a more round face, seeming to take his cue from Dr Donnai.

I was curious about Dr Donnai's role in the situation as I knew that he and the obstetrician who had overseen my pregnancy were both through their individual Health Authorities being taken to court over another case; and I had called into question whether this made him an *independent* expert.

He was also married to Dr Dian Donnai, who we had been referred to for genetic counselling. Although this didn't concern us; we wondered whether he had or would discuss our situation with his wife.

Both doctors were throughout the day polite and professional in listening to our grievances and answering our questions as best they could.

At lunchtime, we caught a glimpse of Dr Donnai leaning against the building outside, dragging heavily on a cigarette, looking tired; and momentarily we felt sorry for him having to perform this task, as after all what had happened was nothing to do with him.

Once back in the room that afternoon we clashed with both these doctors, and any earlier sympathy disappeared as we realised that they were only executing the jobs which they had been trained for, and for which they were presumably being very well paid.

Nonetheless, by the end of the day they looked as tired as we felt as we made our way home. We were so tired that we scarcely had energy to discuss whether we felt the meeting had been worthwhile, but eventually concluded that we didn't expect anything to come from this; although it had allowed us to fully air our grievances as to how my pregnancy and

Gregory's birth had been handled.

We felt confident that Miss Bannister had honestly told us as much as she could about Gregory, so tried to resume some semblance of normality, trying to throw ourselves into our home life and work, seemingly with little success.

As the anniversary of Gregory's birth approached, we both felt as despondent as ever. As the day drew ever closer, I began to think that we wouldn't get through it. It was almost as though we expected something cataclysmic to happen we held the date in such dread.

Scarcely eating, sleeping, or even communicating with each other now, we decided that we needed to get away. We didn't want any family or friends trying to comfort us, as we felt that there was no comfort to be had. With these thoughts in mind, we booked a short break in The Lake District.

We felt no happier away than at home.

It was at this time that Margaret Thatcher's long, indomitable reign as Britain's first female Prime Minister, was coming to a calamitous end. We watched the TV as one after another her Ministers abandoned her.

On Gregory's birthday, we decided that we could not dwell on the sadness of what had happened to him, but that we should celebrate his life. After all, the more time that passed, the more we realised just how much he had meant to us.

We celebrated his life with a meal in a quiet Greek restaurant. Returning to our room, having eating a good meal and raised a glass to toast Gregory's life we tumbled into bed for a rest, and for the first time in months made love.

Instinct told me that this was a special time, that something monumental had happened. For a moment I didn't know what this was.

A minute later, with a thumping heart but also sure of my instinct, I told Ross that we had conceived our second child.

In silence, but with a stunned look on his face, he turned on the television to special news reports of Margaret Thatcher bidding farewell to Downing Street; tears rolling down her cheeks. The 'iron lady' was crying, an unprecedented scoop for the media recording her every move.

It was a momentous time in history.

We wept too, not only for the past, but also for the future. Although accepting that this next pregnancy would not be easy; that we had many hurdles to overcome, with perhaps difficult decisions to be faced, we felt that we were strong enough to get through it together.

And although we hadn't even particularly discussed whether or not we should try for another child, we understood that Gregory had been a gift from nature; and as such, we both instinctively knew that our lives would not be worthwhile for either of us without a family.

For the first time, I felt that Gregory's life had been for a reason.

Gregory was the foundation stone upon which we built our family.

Report of the Independent Professional Review

It was the 4th January 1991, when we finally received the Report, through the Mersey Regional Health Authority, written by the independent experts who had conducted the Review. A statement signed by these professionals indicated that the report was dictated on 1st November 1990; with Dr P Donnai initially dictating the first part, followed by comments from Dr P D Edwards.

It is reproduced as written in full here, following the layout in which it was typed.

'Independent Professional Review

Ms. Francesca Nield

Review held at Macclesfield Hospital on Thursday, 1st November 1990

During her first pregnancy in 1989 Ms. Nield was booked for ante-natal care on a shared care basis. She attended the peripheral Knutsford Clinic at 10 weeks gestation. Her medical history was taken by a midwife and certain pre-natal tests discussed. Ms. Nield gave a distant family history on her husband's side of spina bifida. It was not felt this substantially contributed to the risks in the current pregnancy. She apparently discussed the question of amniocentesis with the midwife who advised against this in terms of her

283

age, she being only 32 years of age. The midwife also handed the patient a form concerning the early detection of open spina bifida which clearly pointed out that the serum alpha feto-protein (AFP) investigation only identified 70 – 75% of these cases.

Ms. Nield returned to the clinic at 16 weeks having had an ultrasound scan performed. This apparently revealed no abnormality and at about that time, the serum AFP measurement was performed, which was likewise normal. At 32 weeks gestation, a further scan was performed for foetal growth only. The measurements reveal a normal biparietal diameter and trunk-circumference. There is no comment with regard to excess amniotic fluid and no reason to assume that the foetal spinal (*sic*) was studied in detail. At 37 weeks gestation Ms. Nield was examined by Dr. Scott. There was no clinical evidence for hydramnios and a nitrazine swab taken to test for premature rupture of the membranes was negative. Ms. Nield was admitted briefly at 39 weeks because of back ache and pelvic pain. This may well have been due to a urinary tract infection, successfully treated with Amoxil by the General Practitioner following the finding of haematuria. Ms. Nield was in hospital overnight and discharged the following day. She was not actually seen by the Consultant but the midwives apparently were quite happy with her condition and the Consultant was aware of the clinical situation.

Ms. Nield was subsequently admitted in labour 1 week later at 39 weeks gestation. There were apparently difficulties in attaching a foetal heart electrode. These were resolved by the Acting Registrar, Dr. Murphy, who then decided that in view of the foetal heart decelerations noted that caesarean section was indicated.

An emergency caesarean section was subsequently performed under general anaesthesia, no technical difficulty was encountered, but the baby was floppy at delivery and handed immediately to the Paediatrician on call for resuscitation.

Dictation by Dr. Edwards, Consultant Paediatrician

The new born baby was handed by Dr. Murphy, Obstetric Registrar to a scrubbed nurse who subsequently handed the baby to Dr. Dempsey, Paediatric S.H.O. who placed the infant on the resuscitator. The baby required immediate ventilation which was carried out promptly and satisfactorily. Following the significant improvement in the baby's condition he was extubated, but in view of the initial problem, was transferred personally by Dr. Dempsey to the Special Care Baby Unit. On arrival there, it was noted that his condition deteriorated, by which time Dr. Shackleton arrived on the Special Care Unit and saw his condition. Re-intubation was difficult and was effected by an Anaesthetist. Initial investigations revealed the baby to be markedly acidotic PH6.71 and extremely floppy.

Ventilation was successfully established, the baby was examined by Dr. Shackleton who found no obvious abnormality, but in view of her clinical feeling that the baby would require long term ventilation, she summoned the Paediatric Flying Squad from Crewe, at which hospital long term ventilation is carried out in this part of the Mersey Region. Prior to transfer, the baby's overall condition had improved, confirmed by a PH measurement of 7.4. When the baby was transferred from the Resuscitaire (*sic*) in the Special Baby Unit to the transport ventilator incubator brought from Crewe, it was noted that the baby had a 3 cm x 3 cm lumbosacral meningomyelocele open in the centre. At that time, it was noted that the head circumference at 35 cm is on the 50th centile for a term male infant, i.e. normal.

Following the discovery of the neural tube problem, transfer was arranged to Booth Hall Children's Hospital rather than Crewe, and subsequent care of the baby was undertaken by Miss Bannister, Consultant Neuro-Surgeon. We have not enquired into the subsequent clinical course at that hospital, it being beyond the remit of this review. We are, of course, aware of the fact that the infant died at that hospital.

Comment

The following episodes in Ms. Nield's obstetric care were discussed.

1. The distant family history of spina bifida – this was not thought to be relevant.

2. It was agreed that there was no specific indication for amniocentesis although Ms. Nield requested one initially.

3. The limitations of ultrasound scanning were clearly discussed with Ms. Nield and her partner. It was pointed out that even in the very best centres, currently, at least 5% of neural tube abnormalities will be missed. Ms. Nield was somewhat unhappy with this statement, inasmuch as she felt the majority of those lesions would be the very small, and possibly inconsequential ones. It was pointed out that this failure of ultrasound detection, in fact, also related to more major lesions. Dr. Edwards and I both felt that in all probability, at the time of the alpha feto protein estimation the lesion may well have been closed and that amniocentesis would not have been of help, 20% of open lesions being associated with a normal serum AFP level.

4. It was pointed out that the 32 week scan was performed for foetal growth only, this being Mrs. Scott's practice and one that is widely adopted nationally.

5. Mrs. Scott was able to reassure us that she had clinically assessed the liquor volume and found no evidence of hydramnios.

6. Ms. Nield was critical of her reception in the hospital on several occasions, both at the time of the 16 week scan and again when admitted as an urgency at 39 weeks. Similarly, in labour, she encountered difficulties in communication with medical and nursing staff. This seems to have been a fairly common pattern throughout her pregnancy. We cannot comment more specifically on these inter-personal interactions.

7. We were able to clarify that Dr. Murphy, not unreasonably, made the diagnosis of foetal distress at an early stage of labour and quite appropriately, in our opinion, proceeded to an emergency caesarean section. This was performed without technical difficulty and Dr. Murphy was able to reassure us that the immediate resuscitation of the neonate was performed promptly and expeditiously by the resident Paediatrician.

Paediatric Comment – Dr. Edwards

1. **Resuscitation**

The resuscitation of the baby was discussed with Ms. Nield. It is our feeling that the resuscitation was carried out promptly and effectively and we believe that she accepted that point of view.

2. **Discovery of Meningomyelocele**

The late discovery of this lesion is regrettable. This expression was used in discussion with Ms. Nield. It was however pointed out that immediately upon discovery of the lesion at the age of some 2 ½ hours, Dr. Shackleton immediately went to see the parents, informed them of the presence of the lesion and indeed apologised for its late discovery. This point was accepted by Ms. Nield in discussion.

3. **Natural History of Condition**

It was pointed out to Ms. Nield that the late discovery of this lesion, as noted earlier, did not however, in any way, alter the natural clinical history of her infant son and with this she also agreed, whilst commenting that it had caused adverse psychological effect on her and her husband.

4. **Hydrocephalus**

There was no clinical evidence of hydrocephalus at Macclesfield as evidenced by the head circumference which lay on the 50th centile accompanied by Dr. Shackleton's comment that the clinical impression of tension in the anterior fontanelle was normal. The head circumference measurement is confirmed at Booth Hall. Dr. Shackleton's clinical impression is confirmed in a discharge/death letter, written to Dr. Shackleton, by Miss Bannister, Consultant Neurosurgeon, Manchester. This interpretation by Miss Bannister, however, was disputed by Ms. Nield.

5. The baby's severe general initial condition was pointed out to Ms. Nield and the fact that resuscitation had been extremely effective at Macclesfield. This, I believe, was accepted by her.

6. The assumption is made that the baby's respiratory problems were caused by the significant hydrocephalus with probably mid brain compression. However, in the absence of a post mortem examination, consent for which was refused by the parents, this is an assumption and clearly the presence of other major congenital malformations cannot be totally excluded.

Recommendations

1. We feel that the limitations of pre-natal tests should be more clearly defined and the limitations communicated clearly to the patients, particularly if they agree to undertake such tests.

2. It should be recognised that when sensitive pre-natal tests such as ultrasound scanning are performed, the ambience within which these procedures are performed must naturally be relaxed and sensitive to the patient's needs. This does not always seem to have been the case.

3. There is clearly a need to ensure that junior staff are familiar with the foetal monitoring equipment. This certainly appears not to have been the case when Ms. Nield was admitted in early labour with ruptured membranes, difficulties being encountered in obtaining appropriate electrodes etc. for foetal monitoring.

Paediatric Recommendations

1. As mentioned earlier, it is to be regretted that the discovery of the meningomyelocele was delayed. Clearly, it would be highly desirable to eliminate such a future occurrence. Its avoidance can only occur by the continual stressing

of good clinical practice. However, in this individual case, we found no evidence of improper clinical practice, bearing in mind the baby's significant poor condition at birth. Clearly, it is desirable that a baby is fully examined as soon as practicable within the constraints of other problems.

2. Many of Ms. Nield's difficulties, certainly after the delivery of the baby, relate to communication with staff on the Special Care Unit and her own and her husband's visits to the Special Care Unit.

Many of these could be avoided by structural modifications in the layout at Macclesfield. We believe that some modifications have been undertaken and indeed have been pressed for by consultant medical staff over many years without success and we would strongly re-enforce (*sic*) their desire that an efficient modern obstetric/neo-natal unit be provided.

Conclusion

Firstly, regrettable though the sequence of events may be that overtook Ms. Nield and her pregnancy, we both find no evidence of sub-standard care in that the actions taken through the pregnancy and after delivery were all understandable and appropriate at the various times. The limitations of those procedures have, however, been discussed above.

In conclusion, Dr. Edwards and I both feel that Ms. Nield and her partner remain dissatisfied. They agreed in some small way, our discussions have been of help, but overall, they both remain disillusioned with medicine and its practitioners; and are dismayed by the rare limitations that may be demonstrated. This case has been the subject of several reviews, and as far as we can ascertain, all reasonable points that require discussion have been analysed carefully.'

Family

**Life
Death**

Life *and* Death.

**Birth
Death**

Birth *and* Death?

There are few *certainties* in life. Once born, the only common factor which we *all* share seems to be *death*.

And yet, surprisingly, our society does not prepare us for this.

It is certainly no part of the preparations for birth.

And, arguably, it should not be so. Birth is a time for celebration, an affirmation of the miracle of life. Little wonder then that when the natural order of the world is turned upon its head, no one knows how to cope, or what to say.

This is the situation we found ourselves in.

And even my body was confused.

I had given birth, and accordingly my body was following nature's course to look after the newborn. My body didn't register that my baby had died. Everything about it changed now to nurture and care for a *living* baby.

If nature behaves in such a way – little wonder then that as human beings we are so emotionally and intellectually unequipped to cope with such loss.

The cruel quirks of nature

Nothing could have prepared us for what happened.

And in a sense, we are still after all this time reeling from what happened to us.

Obviously though, life does go on. Although our lives now lay in tatters, it was business as usual for everybody else. Long after the news of our tragedy had circulated throughout our community, and condolences and expressions of sympathy had been made, we felt different – permanently changed, but everything else carried on as usual.

Such is life.

And thus I learned how insignificant I am - indeed, we *all* are - in the grand scheme of things. *Thus, I learned my role in the Universe.*

Although a bitter blow I have always accepted that *we* conceived a disabled baby. For us, this fact was never in dispute. We accepted the extent of Gregory's disabilities as soon as they were known; although for me instinct had kicked in long before we had been given an accurate assessment of his problems.

What we both found difficult to come to terms with was the poor standard of care which both Gregory and I had received, and we felt a huge sense of disappointment at the aloof and dispassionate attitude of some of the medical profession. I am sure that if we hadn't received the support of Miss Bannister - Gregory's neurosurgeon, that I would be bitter until this day about this.

As it was, after the Independent Professional Review there seemed little more that we could do; to either extract an apology for how events had transpired for us, or to seek to ensure that the same thing didn't happen to anyone else.

One good thing which did come out of the situation was that it stirred some of the midwives at Macclesfield into action. They demanded that a private room be set aside for any parents who were having a difficult time in pregnancy or labour, and the administration agreed to this, telling us that we should recognise this as a tribute to our son.

The midwives approached a local furniture company – Arighi Bianchi in Macclesfield, and they provided comfortable furniture with which to furnish this room; so that it was like a room in a hotel, instead of a hospital. Watching the regional news on TV one evening, I felt a cold shiver run down my back as I watched a report about this. It was a small and bitter sweet victory; but I was pleased to think that at least *someone* had done *something* to try to change the situation for others.

As far as we were concerned, we both still felt that there was a lot we didn't know about aspects of what had happened, so I decided to use my law degree to put pressure on Mersey Regional Health Authority to release mine and Gregory's medical notes. This they duly did: now placing the matter in the hands of their solicitors.

Reading the notes was very upsetting, but nonetheless it helped us to understand how events had evolved; to understand the extent of the mismanagement of my pregnancy from beginning to end: to see how one mistake led to another, leading to a catalogue of errors which snowballed out of control.

We were *devastated* to read how many times Gregory had been intubated; and on how many occasions this had been difficult, and I felt that even if Gregory had not been damaged with spina bifida that he could/would have been brain damaged by this.

There was a letter from the obstetrician in the notes stating that she had a scanned image revealing Gregory's spine to be normal. We haven't seen this; which led us to question whether we had received *all* of the notes, or selected notes only.

What the notes did reveal was the length to which each individual member of the medical profession had gone to ensure that they wouldn't be blamed for anything which had gone wrong.

The obstetrician and paediatrician blamed the midwife at booking clinic for not making a note about the family history of spina bifida which I had given when she initially booked my pregnancy. Letters between the medical staff and administrators revealed how much at loggerheads they were concerning the provision of services and beds.

The worst aspect of reading the notes concerned what we read about the paediatrician.

Although we had never sought to castigate her for not examining Gregory; and thus possibly preventing events from transpiring as they had, we were surprised to read how ferociously she had acted against *everyone*. Her letters were emotional and irrational, *perhaps indicating just how much she too had been affected by what had happened.*

We also read a long letter of complaint from Leighton Hospital about the fact that the paediatrician had not diagnosed Gregory's spina bifida at Macclesfield; and as a consequence had created problems at Leighton by taking up *their* staffs' precious time and resources. Apparently, it was mid-afternoon by the time they were able to return from Booth Hall Children's Hospital in Manchester to resume their own work at their own hospital.

Letters had passed between the paediatrician and the administrators at Macclesfield which were overtly blunt - to say the least. The paediatrician blamed lack of resources for what had happened; and the administrators called into question her medical skills.

Most upsetting, from our point of view, were accusations levelled at us by the paediatrician: which had not been aired when we met in person; and which were ludicrous and refutable, but nonetheless hurt us to the core. She criticised our motives for complaining, stating that we were looking for someone to blame because we had had a disabled baby.

Amongst other extremely personal criticisms, she suggested things which could be used against us; such as checking whether we were actually married, whether the baby was planned, and if we were the sort of people who could cope with a handicapped child. She contacted the Medical Defence Union for support, and tried to prevent the Independent Professional Review.

The Medical Defence Union replied in a letter to her (about me):

'...
it would appear that she is not being highly critical of your own department. I think that it is right that the clinical aspects of the matter are being referred for independent professional review since the claimant has not been satisfied by the first stage of the complaints procedure. I do not anticipate that you would have difficulties with the review. I appreciate that there may be some concern that the spina bifida was not immediately recognised, but, as you say, the paediatricians were much concerned with the resuscitation of the infant.

I would be happy to discuss the case further should you require.'

The letter was signed by Dr. J. Gilberthorpe.

When Ross saw the notes he was very angry at what he read and decided himself to write a letter to everyone who had been involved in our care, bringing a close to any further communication on the matter, in which he stated:

'...

The key clinical staff involved, ... failed to identify the essence of Francesca's complaint. If this has not been clear before, then I hope I have clarified it here. Throughout her complaint Francesca has essentially strived to simply establish the events of, and where possible to understand what went wrong with the management of her pregnancy and during Gregory's first hours. If as a result of these enquiries any people who were involved come to the conclusion that "they are to blame" then that is a matter for their own conscience. ...'

And, so far as we were concerned, we had established as many facts as we could to determine where or how things had gone wrong and determined that there was nothing more we could do about it, although I did write a final letter to the Health Authority's solicitor outlining where I believed there had been negligence. If Gregory had lived, I expect that we would have found ourselves in the situation which so many other parents find themselves – the stressful and long struggle of having to sue to help with the large costs associated with bringing up a disabled child.

As it was, Gregory was dead, and there was nothing that we could do to change this situation. We would have to find a way to learn to live with it.

For us, having had such a beautiful son - albeit for such a short time, we didn't feel that we would be able to move forward without a family. We briefly discussed the idea of adoption, but quickly dismissed this, deciding that it was our own children we wanted.

Armed with the advice we had received at the genetic counselling clinic and taking Pregnavite Forte F and *extra* folic acid, we decided that we would let nature take its course. Becoming pregnant with our second child on what would have been Gregory's first birthday felt very special.

I had been advised by Dr Dian Donnai, the geneticist, that any further pregnancies would be more carefully monitored and that the best place for this to happen would be at St Mary's Hospital for women and children in Manchester. The geneticist was the wife of Mr Paul Donnai, the obstetrician who had participated in the Independent Professional Review and worked at St Mary's. Feeling that he would have an in-depth knowledge of what had happened in my previous pregnancy, I asked him whether he would act as my obstetrician in the present one. He seemed surprised when I asked, but immediately agreed to do so.

I received our notes from the Health Authority in the spring of 1991, and was deeply distressed to read what Gregory in particular had gone through. As my second child fluttered gently inside me, I stroked my abdomen, wondering what lay in store for us now. Still grieving for Gregory, I determined to take one day at a time, and to again enjoy this new pregnancy.

Although this pregnancy should/could have been more stressful than my first, it was made easier by the high standard of medical attention that I received. This time I didn't share care with a GP practice, but saw Mr Donnai exclusively at the hospital in Manchester. He was kindness itself from beginning to end. Other than the scans I saw him at every appointment, never being left in the hands of any other doctor or midwife. He instilled in me a quiet confidence that whatever the situation, that it would be dealt with professionally and sympathetically. He personally performed an amniocentesis test, and arranged for me to receive a detailed fetal anomaly scan, performed by a specialist radiographer; even sending me for a second expert opinion at another hospital, as I was scared to believe that this baby didn't have spina bifida: the first detailed scan showing that we were expecting a healthy baby boy.

As the pregnancy progressed, I discussed with Mr Donnai what sort of birth I should have, and we both agreed that the sensible option in view of what had happened last time was for an elective caesarean section, performed under epidural, with me being awake and involved at all times with what was going on. Towards the end of the pregnancy, as I ballooned in weight and my blood pressure became slightly elevated I was taken into hospital for observation.

I spent approximately four weeks there before delivery, although I was allowed home for a day at the weekends. I was given my own room with en-suite facilities and was seen on a regular basis by Mr Donnai. Finally, he decided that it was time to deliver the baby. He introduced me to the anaesthetist, and whilst I

302

was being administered the epidural he scrubbed up and waited in theatre for us. With Ross standing by my side, holding my hand, and numerous other theatre staff on hand, I saw in the steel rim of the theatre light Mr Donnai make his first incision. As quiet music played in the background, I was terrified that something would go wrong. After feeling what felt like tugs and rummaging - felt as strong but not painful sensations, I saw over the green tarpaulin cloth, cutting off the view below my waist, a baby's body, curled and purple as a frozen turkey, being lifted out.

I felt that I stopped breathing, and it was as though time stood still as the cord was cut and the baby quickly checked. For a moment there was no cry, and as Ross and I exchanged looks of despair, the paediatrician walked over with him and placed him in our arms. If Gregory had been beautiful, Alistair was equally so, and the pleasure we felt at his birth, although tinged with sadness at the loss of Gregory, was scarcely credible. This time I felt like pinching myself, feeling overwhelmed by a beautiful dream instead of the nightmare I had previously experienced.

A couple of months after Alistair's birth we read a paper in *Chemistry in Britain* detailing the benefits for women who were planning a pregnancy of taking a folic acid supplement prior to conception. Shortly afterwards, Liam Donaldson, the Government's Spokesman for Health, made an announcement backing this.

Sad that this information had been made public too late to help Gregory, we were pleased to know that there was a lot women could now do to help prevent babies being conceived with spina bifida.

Alistair was an easy and a happy baby, but we didn't want him to be an only child; particularly as we didn't intend to conceal from him the fact that he had had an older brother, feeling that this could make him a lonely, solitary child. In view of the fact that Mr Donnai had promised that he would look after me in the same way as he had when I had been pregnant with Alistair, once I had breast fed Alistair for several months I changed him to formula milk, and after taking supplements of folic acid, we decided that we should now try to complete our family by having another child.

Although Alistair was only six months old I felt that if we were to have another child that I would have to get on with this, feeling that if we left it for any time that I would lose all confidence and never try again for another baby.

Throughout my next pregnancy, I again received the same standard of care from Mr Donnai which I had received with Alistair - and for which I shall forever be indebted to him for. At all times he showed professionalism combined with extreme kindness in his dealings, not only towards me, but Ross also.

Rachel was born on 23 November 1992, again by elective caesarean section personally performed by Mr Donnai - who again used the same anaesthetist, to the strains of Handel's *Water Music* - one day after what would have been Gregory's third birthday.

The birth of our beautiful daughter completed our family.

It is difficult to put into words what family has meant to us. It has taken us to the very depths of despair, but has also brought us immeasurable happiness.

As a mother, Gregory's loss sits on my shoulder as a constant companion. I loved him as our first child, and know that I will never completely come to terms with his loss, no matter how much time passes.

Despite the fact that it is so long since he was born and died, every year as the anniversaries approach, I feel as though I become *disconnected* from events going on around me in some way. Once more, I recall all the details of what happened at that time, and as the leaves turn and fall from the trees, I feel overwhelmingly sad.

Friends gave us a maple tree which we planted at the bottom of the garden in memory of Gregory. This tree has grown from a sapling to a large straight tree which stands solid, holding its own against the winter winds; beautiful and perfectly shaped crimson leaves clinging tenaciously to its branches long after most other trees have shed theirs.

At this time, I see Gregory everywhere. As clouds roll across a dark sky they change into the shape of my baby. The water in puddles of rain pools in such a way that they reflect back to me the shape of his beautiful body. I feel as though he is around me everywhere; and yet I feel as though I am constantly searching for him.

I become more fearful at this time of year. Although I know that I am thinking irrationally and being controlled by grief, I see fear lurking around every corner. I see it in ordinary situations, and understand that this is the legacy I have been left with.

I feel that the way that events unfolded in my pregnancy with Gregory has robbed me of any sense of peace of mind, however much time passes. I am now keenly aware of how quickly life can change; from everything seeming to be normal, to disaster striking in an instant.

I have total, and, I believe, accurate recall of events as they happened. I have repeatedly questioned why I can't let Gregory go, and feel that this is because I do not want to do so.

Perhaps this is why I have written his story. In the depths of despair after Gregory's death I lamented the fact that he should have been born only to know suffering, and Miss Bannister at this time instilled in me the belief that every life, however short or difficult, is for a reason, and over the years I have held onto this thought.

It not only provided some comfort where there seemed none to be had in the early days, but it later encouraged me to think about the positives which have resulted from Gregory's birth and death. The first is that I hope by writing this book that other parents suffering any aspect of the difficulties we encountered may be helped in some small way by me sharing our experiences.

Most important of all, I believe that what happened has made me appreciate the value of my family and has enabled me to enjoy them more than I perhaps might have done. The counterview to this is that perhaps it has made me a more cautious mother who worries too much about her other children, although I understand that this is unquantifiable; although I do know that on occasions over the years that in so far as my other children are concerned that my rational thoughts can so very easily be overwhelmed by a fear of calamity lurking round every corner waiting for them.

I have so little left of Gregory – only his ashes, a hat donated to the hospital which he wore when he died, and the photographs which we took of him. Initially I hated this acrylic hat with the label N.M.G.H.A., beneath which there are the letters, S.C.B.U. stamped on it (North Manchester General Health Authority, Special Care Baby Unit) but over the years I have gained some comfort from it as I recall him wearing it. I now treasure this hat and the photographs, which I have put into a new album as the old one became tatty.

On his birthday, I like to look at his photographs, although I don't really need to as his image is indelibly imprinted on my mind. Sometimes I will sleep with the hat under my pillow, sniff it, or hold it against my cheek. It has become precious.

I do not fear losing sight of how he looked and felt as some bereaved do. Perhaps this is because he will never change. Looking back at photos of my other two children, I am surprised by how much they have changed, and by how quickly they do so.

Sometimes, the cold finger of loss can squeeze so tight that it seems to squeeze the very life out of me; and as I watch the other children I regret that Gregory hasn't had the same opportunities as them. At other times I can watch my other two children grow and mature, and I feel as though I could burst with pride. This, Gregory, is the legacy which you left me – an appreciation of, and an overwhelming sense of love and pride in, my family.

I feel that there is nothing more that I can add but this – that I will never forget you Gregory, you were and always will be our first child, an integral part of our family, and I will always remember you; and completing your story, I would like to sign off with the words – *all my love, mum.*

Appendix 1

Gregory

Our first child, Gregory, was born on 22 November and died three days later, having been born with spina bifida and hydrocephalus. He was on a life support machine throughout his short life and had two operations, one to insert a shunt, and the other to cover the spina bifida on his back so that it should not become infected.

My pregnancy had been an easy and a happy one. There had been no signs that there were any problems and I had felt well throughout, and after two scans and all the other routine tests, had been confident that the baby was healthy. Nothing could have prepared me for what happened.

Gregory was delivered by emergency caesarean section in a small maternity unit and was thereafter transferred to a hospital in Manchester, where he was operated upon and nursed until his death.

The neurosurgeon told my husband and me on the morning of Gregory's death that the part of our baby's brain which controlled breathing had either not fully developed or was damaged and that he would never be able to breathe for himself. We asked that he be taken off the life support machine immediately and that he be allowed to die in peace with us.

Though shocked, we fully appreciated everything that was happening at that time, but could not grasp the enormity of the situation. We had touched and talked to Gregory during his time on the life support machine and had been encouraged by staff to participate in his nursing and had washed and changed him. We had also taken photographs, not realising at the time just how important they were to be to us.

When we knew that he was going to die, mixed with the sense of shock and sorrow was a feeling of anticipation, that at last we would be able to cuddle him without all the constrictions of the life support machinery, which over the last few days had acted as a barrier between us.

There was an urgency about the situation, a compelling need to convey to him our feelings for him, to cram a lifetime of love and care into a few precious minutes. And so we kissed and cuddled Gregory until he died, and took more photographs. We can only hope that Gregory's last few moments were ones of comfort and love, as I feel sure had been the time during the nine months I had carried him. Previously, had I been called upon to imagine the situation in the hospital when he died, I might have thought it bizarre or morbid even. Now to me, the memories are precious. I recall looking out of the window as Gregory died, and saw that the sun was shining. Both our families, who had been supportive since his birth, came to the hospital to say goodbye to him, arriving before he died or very shortly afterwards.

Gregory died with a peaceful look on his face, a look captured forever. My husband, who works as a research scientist for a photographic company, developed the photographs himself that he had taken, which gave him a sense of doing something positive and meaningful after Gregory's death, when we were so consumed with grief.

Now, we cannot imagine how we would feel if we didn't have the photographs to remind us of how he looked. My favourite is one taken after his death, where his expression is one of the utmost peace and which shows just what a beautiful baby he was. The cruel blow smote by nature in his development is compensated for by his beauty and in the fact that he was in a physical sense so perfectly formed. The photographs capture all of this and now bring to mind not only the way he looked, but how he felt to touch. We couldn't have imagined that events would take the course that they did at the outset of my pregnancy and are still grappling with the enormity of what has happened and grieving for our son, but there are things which sustain us: the photographs, which even at the blackest of times bring back the good memories; the recollections of my pregnancy and the expectations and excitement of that time, which, although dashed, can never be taken away from us; and above all, the fact that we had such a beautiful son who will live forever in our hearts and minds.

Of course, we would have wished it different, and still talk of how things should have been, but with time, we are slowly coming to an acceptance of what has happened and draw comfort where we can. I do have one regret, that I didn't keep a lock of Gregory's hair.

I take comfort from a passage in one of

Wordsworth's poems called 'Intimations of Immortality', which will always serve as a reminder of Gregory, as will a tree which friends gave us in his memory and which we planted in our garden as a lasting tribute to the son we loved so much.

Published by the National Childbirth Trust, SANDS and ASBAH*

* Published as 'The loss of a child – *a mother's personal account of bereavement,*' *Link* (The magazine for people with Spina Bifida and/or Hydrocephalus) August 1990, No 129, p18; 'Gregory,' SANDS Newsletter – Spring 1991, pp 4-5; and 'Gregory,' *Brief Lives*, Parents writing about the death of a baby (London, The National Childbirth Trust, 1995), pp 3-4.

Appendix 2

Useful information*

The following are helpful organisations which can provide information and support around pregnancy, childbirth, disability and bereavement. This is by no means a definitive list. It is always useful to consult your local GP/surgery, the Internet, library, or telephone book for information on support groups within your own area and up-to-date information.

ASBAH

The 'Association for Spina Bifida and Hydrocephalus' provided a wealth of information to both individuals and professionals. A network of advisers worked throughout England, Wales and Northern Ireland, advising on all aspects of these disorders. Its registered office is situated at:

42 Park Road
Peterborough
PE1 2UQ
England
(*previously*)
Helpline: 0845 450 7755
email: enquiries@asbah.org
website: http://www.asbah.org

as of 20 October 2011 this became

SHINE

(This year they celebrate 50 years of helping others)

Spina bifida
Hydrocephalus
Information
Networking
Equality

the address remains the same

tel: 01733 555988
website: http://www.shinecharity.org.uk

AvMA

Formerly known as '**Action for Victims of Medical Accidents**' this UK charity can provide useful legal advice on different medical issues, and can advise on specialist legal help in local geographical areas. Visit their website at: http://www.avma.org.uk or use their Helpline: 0845 123 2352.

The Compassionate Friends

The Compassionate Friends is a self support organisation, where bereaved parents and families offer support after the death of a child. Their UK Telephone Helpline, always answered by a bereaved parent, can put you in touch with local support: 0345 123 2304.

Mail enquiries to:
The Compassionate Friends
14 New King St
Deptford
London
SE8 3HS
website: http://www.tcf.org.uk

Cruse Bereavement Care

Offer one to one support or group counselling to anyone who has been affected by a death. Their Helpline is 0808 808 1677.
email: helpline@cruse.org.uk
website: http://www.cruse.org.uk

General Medical Council

The General Medical Council is a registered charity which regulates the medical profession in the UK and licenses doctors to practise. Its aim is to deliver and protect the highest standards of medical ethics, education and practice, in the interest of patients, the public and the profession. It can look into a doctor's fitness to practise. It has offices in:

London
Manchester
Edinburgh
Cardiff
Belfast

website: http://www.gmc-uk.org

International Federation for Spina Bifida and Hydrocephalus

The IF was founded by people with spina bifida and hydrocephalus and families in 1979 as a voluntary association. It has become a professional disabled people's organisation with *global* coverage, democratic structure and transparent and accountable processes. Contact details:

Cellebroersstraat 16/Rue des Alexiens 16
B – 1000
Brussels
Belgium

tel: +32(0) 2 502 0413
email: info@ifglobal.org

NCT

The 'National Childbirth Trust' is the UK's largest parenting charity, providing a wealth of information, counselling and a variety of other support concerning all areas of childbirth. Local branches run ante natal and post natal courses.
website: http://www.nct.org.uk

NHS Organ Donor Register

'UK Transplant' manages the NHS Organ Donor Register. Their website is at: http://www.uktransplant.org.uk The NHS Organ Donor Line is: 0300 123 23 23. For information on helping to save lives by giving blood contact: 0117 975 7575. Organ Donor cards can be picked up at GPs' surgeries and pharmacies. Alternatively, donors can sign up online.

Samaritans

Founded by Chad Varah 55 years ago, this invaluable registered charity now has 202 local branches in the UK and the Republic of Ireland; all manned 24 hours a day by trained volunteers. They provide non-judgmental emotional support on *all* issues. Write to:
Freepost
RSRB-KKBY-CYJK
email: jo@samaritans.org

SANDS

is the acronym for the 'Stillbirth and Neonatal Death Society.' It supports anyone affected by the death of a baby, and provides useful information to individuals and professionals alike. Its Head Office is situated at:
Victoria Charity Centre
11 Belgrave Road
London
SW1V 1RB
Helpline: 020 7436 5881
website: http://www.uk-sands.org

SATFA

Previously known by the acronym SATFA, which stood for 'Support Around Termination for Fetal Abnormality' this registered charity was renamed **ARC** ('Antenatal Results and Choices') in 1998. It offers non-directive support and information. Up-to-date details are:

ARC
345 City Road
London
EC1V 1LR
Helpline: 020 7631 0285
email: arcsatfa@aol.com
website: http://www.arc-uk.org

* All information correct as at April 2016.

Epilogue

Decades on, most of us have access to the Internet in one form or another, and information is readily available at our fingertips.

This is only as credible as its source, and useful if acted upon.

In this book, I have written about our struggle to understand what happened to Gregory pre-Internet, and I feel that I cannot leave without acknowledging the help I have received over the years from different sources; and give an overview of the present situation.

As stated, the book would not have been written without Professor Carys Bannister from Booth Hall Children's Hospital, and I have written about the writing of this in a link www.shinecharity.org.uk/shinestars/our-shine-stars/gregory-nield-fielding shared by Shine Charity, who were formerly ASBAH. I have released some photographs on this link of our time in intensive care. A special thanks to Darren Fower and all at this Charity who have helped over the years. It seems appropriate to publish this book in the same year that this Charity celebrates its 50th Anniversary. Marc Lupson and his team have been working on a Heritage Project due in the summer in celebration.

I also set up a facebook page, Gregory Nield-Fielding, where I attempt to share up-to-date information on aspects of spina bifida and hydrocephalus.

Sadly Carys died in 2010, though for so

many her memory lives on, as does her research and place in medical history.

Booth Hall Children's Hospital was razed to the ground a couple of years ago, despite some very spirited local opposition to this, and a housing estate built in its place. Childrens' services have been centralised in Manchester in a new state of the art hospital.

I touched upon the fact that in 1991 there was a Government announcement which indicated that folic acid supplementation could help women who had previously had a child with a neural tube defect to minimise the risk of a further occurrence. This followed research undertaken by Professor Nicholas Wald and his team - in the UK, who reported that another occurrence could be minimised by around 72% if women took a folic acid supplement prior to conception. It was also suggested that *all* women preparing for pregnancy should take a folic acid supplement to ensure the health of their baby. His research also indicated no adverse health effects from this.

It was distressing that this information wasn't in the public domain when we decided to start a family. Prior to speaking to Carys in early 1990, after Gregory's death, we made several visits to Manchester University Library, where we pored for hours over medical textbooks in our quest to find information about spina bifida and hydrocephalus. Was there a genetic cause, was it environmental; had either of us done something to cause this, were questions which preyed heavily on our minds. Carys told us that there could be a genetic component, it could be as a result of a number of factors; and that at this time research was being undertaken to determine whether the mother's nutritional status was implicated.

Carys was instrumental in not only helping us to understand Gregory's problems, but in talking to us about the benefits of folic acid supplementation in minimising the risk of conceiving a child with a neural tube defect by 72% if a folic acid supplement is taken for three months prior to conception and during early pregnancy.

There are several types of neural tube defects. Gregory had the most serious. Others can be invisible; perhaps only picked up later in life, if at all. Then there are others – which necessitate a lifetime of treatment: but as this is not a medical textbook, it is inappropriate to expand on this here.

What I have found has become of the *utmost importance,* is the role of supplementation with folic acid - *prior to conception,* to minimise the risk of conceiving a baby with a neural tube defect. Neural tube defects develop during the first 28 days of pregnancy before many women are aware that they are pregnant. As approximately 50% of pregnancies are unplanned, and the World Health Organisation has revealed that in the UK large numbers of women of child bearing age are folate deficient, I have long been concerned that something needs to be done about the situation.

I supported Martine Austin when she worked on the Go Folic campaign for Shine

Charity, and now that she, and Jackie Bland, have joined the staff of the International Federation for Spina Bifida and Hydrocephalus, I will continue to support them in their efforts to get the message out there. Renee Jopp from the IF has been invaluable in sharing information with me, so many thanks to her.

Globally, others have acted upon the research, initially undertaken by Professor Wald *in the UK*, and continued elsewhere; with many countries introducing the mandatory fortification of flour with folic acid, with significant reductions in neural tube defects.

Here, and elsewhere in Europe, there has been a reluctance to do this. This is disappointing as there is such a strong body of evidence to indicate the benefits of this. Despite repeated recommendations from the UK's Food Standards Agency and the Scientific Advisory Committee on Nutrition in the UK, subsequent governments have refused to act. It was last considered in March 2016 in the House of Lords, who decided against mandatory fortification of flour with folic acid.

I felt particularly sad on hearing this decision, especially as currently one in every thousand pregnancies in the UK is affected by a neural tube defect – exactly the same statistic as in 1989, when we conceived Gregory. I think that it is a cop out to promise an awareness campaign, especially as so many pregnancies are unplanned: and in my personal view feel that this didn't help in 1991; nor has it subsequently.

I am not alone in feeling disappointed.

Many health professionals are outraged that their recommendations are not being implemented. Scotland is presently thinking of *going it alone* and fortifiying their flour with folic acid.

So much work has been undertaken on this, which could save so much heartache – if only the knowledge was in the *public domain*. There is much to be optimistic about, even for families who have had several affected pregnancies.

In February this year the findings of a trial, published in the *British Journal of Nutrition*, indicate that taking Inositol, also known as vitamin B8, alongside folic acid, may be the most effective way of preventing neural tube defects in women with a history of affected pregnancies. This was a PONTI study (Prevention of Neural Tube defects by Inositol) funded by Sparks (the Children's Medical Research Council) supported by NMR Biomedical Research Centre, Newlife Foundation for Disabled Children and Great Ormond Street Hospital Charity.

Which leads me to question - why isn't more being done to minimise the risk of spina bifida and hydrocephalus, *the most serious common birth defect known to man*?

The research has been done.

The personal is political!

Finally, I feel that I must point out to all the groups presently involved in some amazing work in redefining terminology surrounding disability, that the terms used in the writing of this book were terms used at the time. I apologise if they cause any offence, but it would be less than honest of me to change anything in this account of the life and death of our first child.

Francesca Nield, April 2016
Facebook pages
Francesca Nield
Gregory Nield-Fielding
Twitter
@FNield
LinkedIn
Francesca Nield LLB

Praise for Too Deep for Tears

Leslie Keegan QC

' ... It was a great privilege to read your story and I am certain that it will be a great comfort to others.

I would very much like to be able to use your manuscript to show our pupil barristers the real human suffering that lies behind many of these cases.

I am also called upon from time to time to speak to groups of doctors or medical students on the topic of clinical negligence and I think that many of them would benefit by me reading an extract from your manuscript.

I learned a great deal from my time at AvMA and from having the privilege of working with you and others in similar situations.

It has greatly increased my understanding of clients ....'

former caseworker for AvMA

Dr Lesley Bayliss

' ... I wept often as I read of your distress and sorrow, and the awfulness of it all. ... Through it I relived some of my time at Booth Hall. I was there for 12 months in 1981-82. ... I also walked the long corridors in the middle of the night and

325

covered I.T.U. so as you described your time in the wards I knew exactly the atmosphere which was surrounding you. I remember specific times when I did not know how to cope with or understand how very ordinary mums and dads had to face the ordeal of their children being very ill or dying or not developing normally. Reading your account and especially how you and your husband began to move forward has affected me more than I can put in words. It is very clear that in his few days Gregory was loved by you both, and stays clear in your memory and I feel I have known him in his uniqueness. I feel honoured to have been able to read your book. ...'

our family GP

Printed in Poland
by Amazon Fulfillment
Poland Sp. z o.o., Wrocław